MR. JUSTICE HOLMES AND THE SUPREME COURT

Second Edition

MR. JUSTICE HOLMES AND THE SUPREME COURT

Felix Frankfurter

THE BELKNAP PRESS
OF HARVARD UNIVERSITY PRESS
Cambridge, Massachusetts
1961

"Oliver Wendell Holmes, March 8, 1841–March 6, 1935,"
is reprinted with the permission of Charles Scribner's Sons from
the Dictionary of American Biography, *Supplement One,*
copyright 1944 by the American Council of Learned Societies.

Library of Congress Catalog Card Number 61–16693

Printed in the United States of America

Foreword

In 1938, a year before he was called to the Supreme Court of the United States, Professor Frankfurter delivered three lectures at Harvard on Mr. Justice Holmes. The lectures, conveying with sympathetic insight Holmes's constitutional philosophy, were designed for a general audience and were published in a slender volume by the Harvard University Press. For some time now the book has been out of print and has been well on the way to becoming a collector's item. Meanwhile, in 1944, Mr. Justice Frankfurter wrote for the *Dictionary of American Biography* a remarkably sensitive biographical notice of Holmes, at once more compressed and more comprehensive, viewing Holmes's life in the large, drawing on his published and unpublished writings, and placing him in the perspective of the history of ideas.

The Syndics of the Press, believing that the earlier volume should no longer remain inaccessible, and that it would become all the more meaningful if conjoined with the later essay, sought and obtained the consent of Mr. Justice Frankfurter to bring the two works together in a single volume. The permission of the publishers of the *Dictionary of American Biography* has made it possible to carry out this happily conceived plan.

Although a new generation of readers may attend to the voice of Holmes as to an echo from another age, they will find, as transmitted through these essays, that it has a disturbingly close resonance. For Holmes was concerned in a philosophical way with the recurring contrapuntal themes of government under law: innovation and continuity, popular will and imposed restraints, practical reason and categorical imperatives. Perhaps the fashioning of harmonies from these discordant strains was for Holmes the reflection of an inner resolution he felt bound to achieve from his Civil War days onward, between skepticism and faith.

For the interpreter too, whether he be historian, literary critic, or biographer, there is a resolution to be made, between fidelity and creativity. Mr. Justice Frankfurter has demonstrated how the two qualities are not necessarily opposed, how they may with devoted insight enhance each other. Holmes's light comes to us not through an artless window glass but refracted with enhanced intensity and beauty by a prismatic mind.

PAUL A. FREUND

10 JULY, 1961
HARVARD LAW SCHOOL

Contents

OLIVER WENDELL HOLMES, 1841–1935 1

MR. JUSTICE HOLMES
AND THE SUPREME COURT 37

Introductory 39

I. Property and Society 45

II. Civil Liberties and the Individual 74

III. The Federal System 88

Oliver Wendell Holmes

1841–1935

in Boston and went first to a woman's school there, then to Rev. T. R. Sullivan's, then to E. S. Dixwell's (Private Latin School) and then to College" (O. W. Holmes, Jr.'s College Autobiography, quoted in F. C. Fiechter, "The Preparation of an American Aristocrat," *New England Quarterly*, March 1933).

Holmes was thus rooted in the Puritan tradition and his personal attachment to its meaning and environment went deep. "I love every brick and shingle of the old Massachusetts towns where once they worked and prayed," he said of his Puritan ancestors in one of his frequent references to them, "and I think it a noble and pious thing to do whatever we may by written word and moulded bronze and sculptured stone to keep our memories, our reverence and our love alive and to hand them on to new generations all too ready to forget" ("Ipswich—At the Unveiling of Memorial Tablets," July 31, 1902, *Speeches*, 1913, p. 92). After leaving Boston, he regularly returned to its nearby North Shore to enjoy each year its dunes and rocks and barberry bushes with refreshing devotion. But even as a college student he was a Bostonian apart. Very early his curiosities far transcended his emotional attachments. His own crowd in Boston, though fascinated, were quizzical about him for reasons that were implied in the remark of a leading lawyer who had been a boyhood friend: "I wish Wendell wouldn't play with his mind." From the time—before he was twenty—that he learned from Emerson the lesson of intellectual independence, his quest for understanding was hemmed in neither by geography nor by personal preferences. So whole-souled was his love of country that only fools could misunderstand when he said, "I do not pin my dreams for the future to my country or even to my race. . . . I think it not improbable that man, like the grub that prepares a chamber for the winged thing it never has seen but is to be—that man may have cosmic destinies that he does not understand" ("Law and the Court," *Collected Legal Papers*, 1920, p. 296). New Englander of New Englanders in his feelings all his life, Holmes disciplined himself against any kind of parochialism in his thinking. Because he so completely rid himself of it, he is a significant figure in the history of civilization and not merely a commanding American figure.

As a truth-seeking Puritan, then, he entered Harvard in the fall of 1857. But before he was graduated came the Civil War and Lincoln's call for men. In April 1861 Holmes, just turned twenty, joined the 4th Battalion of Infantry stationed at Fort Independence. On July 10—having in the meantime written and delivered his class poem and been graduated—he was commissioned second lieutenant and on Sept. 4 he started South with his beloved regiment, the 20th Massachusetts, part of the Army of the Potomac, to share, except when disabled, in its notable history (G. A. Bruce, *The Twentieth Regiment of Massachusetts Volunteer Infantry*, 1906). Three times he was put out of action and his war experiences are the stuff of heroic tales. Not unnaturally could his great friend, Sir Frederick Pollock, sixty years later chaffingly suggest to Holmes that he could reinforce his argument "as to the contra-natural selection of war by the example of a certain stray bullet whose deviation by a fraction of an inch would have deprived" the world of all that Holmes's lucky escape gave it (*Holmes-Pollock Letters*, II, 43). His own recital (*Who's Who in America*) gives Holmes's war record with austere completeness: "Served 3 yrs. with 20th Mass. Volunteers, lieutenant to lieutenant colonel; wounded in breast at Ball's Bluff, Oct. 21, 1861, in neck at Antietam, Sept. 17, 1862, in foot at Marye's Hill, Fredericksburg, May 3, 1863; a.-d.-c. on staff Gen. H. G. Wright, Jan. 29, 1864, until mustered out July 17, 1864, with rank of captain."

On his return to Boston invalided from the front, his personal distinction and his war record irresistibly combined to make of him a military hero. Bishop William Lawrence gives the contemporary picture: "I saw him, a young officer, marching off to the front. . . . I watched his record, for we boys were alert to the heroes of those days, and as he was brought back wounded again and again . . . he was seen on the streets in Boston, a handsome invalid, to the great delectation of the girls of the city. He was a romantic hero, built for it" (address of Bishop Lawrence at presentation of portrait of Mr. Justice Holmes, Mar. 20, 1930, *Harvard Alumni Bulletin*, Mar. 27, 1930). What he called a "flamboyant" piece (*Holmes-Pollock Letters*, II, 270) in *Harper's Weekly* of Nov. 9, 1861, and Dr. Holmes's famous but too stylized *Atlantic Monthly* (December 1862) account of the Antietam episode, "My Hunt after 'the Captain,' " extended young Holmes's martial reputation much beyond the confines of Boston. He himself harbored no romantic notions about war. He saw too much of it. Indeed, he shocked patriotic sentimentalists by speaking of war as an "organized bore," just as later he was to offend those whom he regarded as social sentimentalists by his insistence that war is merely a phase of that permanent struggle which is the law of life. "War, when you are at it, is horrible and dull. It is only when time has passed that you see that its message was divine. I hope it may be long before we are called again to sit at that master's feet. But some teacher of the kind we all need. In this smug, over-safe corner of the world we need it, that we may realize that our comfortable routine is no eternal necessity of things, but merely a little space of calm in the midst of the tempestuous untamed streaming of the world, and in order that we may be ready for danger. We need it in this time of individualist negations, with its literature of French and American humor, revolting at discipline, loving fleshpots, and denying that anything is worthy of reverence,—in order that we may remember all that buffoons forget. We need it everywhere and at all times" ("The Soldier's Faith," a Memorial Day address, May 31, 1895, *Speeches*, pp. 62–63).

These are the convictions he took out of the Civil War. These were the convictions that dominated him for the long years to come For the Civil War probably cut more deeply than any other influence in his life. If it did not generate it certainly fixed his conception of man's destiny. "I care not very much for the form if in some way he has learned that he cannot set himself over against the universe as a rival god, to criticize it, or to shake his fist at the skies, but that his meaning is its meaning, his only worth is as a part of it, as a humble instrument of the universal power" (*Collected Legal Papers*, p. 166). "Life is a roar of bargain and battle, but in the very heart of it there rises a mystic spiritual tone that gives meaning to the whole" (*Speeches*, p. 97). "It is enough for us that the universe has produced us and has within it, as less than it, all that we believe and love. If we think of our existence not as that of a little god outside, but as that of a ganglion within, we have the infinite behind us. It gives us our only but our adequate significance. . . . If our imagination is strong enough to accept the vision of ourselves as parts inseverable from the rest, and to extend our final interest beyond the boundary of our skins, it justifies the sacrifice even of our lives for ends outside of ourselves" (*Collected Legal Papers*, p. 316).

This faith he expressed as a returning soldier and he repeated it, in enduring phrases endlessly varied, for seventy years—in talk, in letters, in speeches, in opinions. But his "Soldier's Faith" was not merely an eloquent avowal of his philosophic beliefs regarding man's destiny, nor was it a gifted man's expression, in emotionally charged phrases, of what seemed to him "the key to intellectual salvation" as well as "the key to happiness" (*Collected Legal Papers*, p. 166). Holmes lived his faith. It would be difficult to conceive a life more self-conscious of its directions and more loyal in action to the faith which it espoused. His faith determined the very few personal choices he was called upon to make after he left the army; it was translated into concreteness in the multifarious cases that came before him for judgment for half a century.

He left the army because his term was up. In later life he said that if he had to do it again he would have stayed through the war. Instead, in the fall of 1864, he began the study of law. On graduating from the Harvard Law School in 1866, he made the first of his numerous visits to England. He had of course easy access to eminent Britishers but he won his way among them, even in his twenties, on his own intellectual distinction. Thus he met some of the great figures of the day—John Stuart Mill, Sir Henry Maine, Benjamin Jowett, the Master of Balliol—and in course of time formed friendships with Leslie Stephen, James Bryce, A. V. Dicey, Sir Frederick Pollock and with gifted women like Mrs. J. R. Green, Mrs. W. K. Clifford, and Miss Beatrice Chamberlain. That a gay, handsome young man with a brilliant tongue—"that lanky talker of a Wendell Holmes"—was the way an old servant in a Beacon Hill household described him—moved easily in English fashionable society is not surprising. Much more significant is the tender friendship that grew between him and an Irish parish priest, Canon Sheehan, whom he met on one of his English visits. Indeed, his last trip to England, in 1913, was made largely to see his friend, who was a-dying. Canon Sheehan, he wrote, "was a dear friend of mine—odd as it seems that a saint and a Catholic should take up with a heathen like me" (unpublished MS., May 19, 1917; see H. J. Heuser, *Canon Sheehan of Doneraile,* 1917). The most intimate of his English ties came to be with Sir Frederick Pollock. Their friendship was maintained by a steady exchange of letters over nearly sixty years. These happily, were preserved, and their publication, thanks to the careful editing of Mark DeWolfe Howe, furnishes a cultural document of first importance for its era (*Holmes-Pollock Letters: The Correspondence of Mr. Justice Holmes and Sir Frederick Pollock, 1874–1932*, 2 vols., 1941).

England had a strong pull for Holmes. "I value everything that shows the quiet unmelodramatic power to stand and take it in your people," wrote Holmes to Pollock early in the First World War (*supra*, I, 222). But he could be sharp in detecting any tendency toward condescension or insensitiveness. He was a proud American who had no sympathy with suggestions of inadequacy of the American environment for finer sensibilities. Thus he thought that "there was a touch of underbreeding" in Henry James's "recurrence to the problem of the social relations of Americans to the old world" (*Ibid.*, II, 41).

After his fling in England, Holmes settled down to the serious business of law. He entered it with strong misgivings and not for years were they quieted. The magnetic disturbance was philosophy. But in 1886, to students whom his old anxieties might beset, he was able to say "no longer with any doubt—that a man may live greatly in the law as elsewhere; that there as well as elsewhere his thought may find its unity in an infinite perspective; that there as well as elsewhere he may wreak himself upon life, may drink the bitter cup of heroism, may wear his heart out after the unattainable" ("The Profession of the Law," *Speeches*, p. 23). Toward the end, when he was past ninety, he put the wisdom of his choice more pungently: "I rather was shoved than went [into the law] when I hankered for philosophy. I am glad now, and even then I had a guess that perhaps one got more from philosophy on the quarter than dead astern" (unpublished letter, June 11, 1931).

In 1867 he was admitted to the bar and practised his profession in Boston, first as an apprentice of Robert M. Morse, then in the office of Chandler, Shattuck & Thayer, and later with George O. Shattuck and William A. Munroe, as a member of the firm of Shattuck, Holmes & Munroe. With fierce assiduity he set himself to become master of his calling. "I should think Wendell worked too hard," wrote William James, in 1869, and the theme recurs in the correspondence of the James family. Holmes never made a fetish of long hours, however; indeed, he believed that what he called work—really creative labor—could not be pursued for more than four hours a day. But he worked with almost feverish intensity. For three years (1870–73), as editor of the *American Law Review*, he ranged the gamut of legal literature—reports, digests, casebooks, revisions of old texts, new treatises, lectures, and essays—and made his own the entire kingdom of law (see *American Law Review*, vols. V–VII, and bibliography in *Harvard Law Review*, March 1931). During the same period he worked indefatigably to bring Kent's *Commentaries* "down through the quarter of a century which has elapsed" since Chancellor Kent's death, and thereby gave new and enduring significance to the most important survey of the earlier American law (see James

Kent, *Commentaries on American Law*, 12th ed., 1873). Holmes thus soaked himself in the details of the law. When he began "the law presented itself as a ragbag of details. . . . It was not without anguish that one asked oneself whether the subject was worthy of the interest of an intelligent man" (*Collected Legal Papers*, p. 301). But his imaginative and philosophic faculties imparted life and meaning to dry details. Where others found only discrete instances he saw organic connection. Thus it was true of him, as he said of another, that his knowledge "was converted into the organic tissue of wisdom" (appreciation of John Chipman Gray reprinted in H. C. Shriver, *Oliver Wendell Holmes: His Book Notices and Uncollected Letters and Papers*, 1936, p. 133). At this time he also lectured on law at Harvard.

During all these years he was in active practice and getting desirable glimpses into actualities. In particular, what it meant to him to be associated with his senior partner, George Otis Shattuck, a leader among Massachusetts lawyers, is the theme of one of his memorable utterances (*Speeches*, pp. 70–74). His temperament being what it was, scholarly pursuits, though a side-line, doubtless enlisted his deepest interests. He would have welcomed appointment to the United States District Court for the greater intellectual freedom it would have afforded him ("The place . . . would enable me to work in the way I want and so I should like it—although it would cost me a severe pang to leave my partners," *Holmes-Pollock Letters*, I, 10). But destiny had other plans for him.

The early writings of Holmes canvassed issues which,

howsoever formulated or disguised, are vital to a society devoted to justice according to law. What are the sources of law and what are its sanctions? What is appropriate lawmaking by courts and what should be left to legislation? What are the ingredients, conscious or unconscious, of adjudication? What are the wise demands of precedent and when should the judicial process feel unbound by its past? Such were the inquiries that guided Holmes's investigations at a time when law was generally treated as a body of settled doctrines from which answers to the new problems of a rapidly industrialized society were to be derived by a process of logical deduction. But in rejecting a view of law which regarded it as a merely logical unfolding Holmes had nothing in common with later tendencies toward a retreat from reason. By disproving formal logic, as the organon of social wisdom he did not embrace antirationalism. Quite the contrary. His faith was in reason and in motives not confined to material or instinctive desires. He refused to believe the theory "that the Constitution primarily represents the triumph of the money power over democratic agrarianism & individualism. . . . I shall believe until compelled to think otherwise that they [the leaders in establishing the Union] wanted to make a nation and invested (bet) or the belief that they would make one, not that they wanted a powerful government because they had invested. Belittling arguments always have a force of their own, but you and I believe that high-mindedness is not impossible to man" (*Ibid.*, II, 222–223). Equally so, while fully aware of the clash of interests in society and of law's mediating function, Holmes had nothing in common with the crude notion according to which law is merely the verbalization of prevailing force and appetites.

But at a time when judges boasted a want of philosophy, Holmes realized that decisions are functions of some juristic philosophy, and that awareness of the considerations that move beneath the surface of logical form is the prime requisite of a civilized system of law. In his analysis of judicial psychology, he was conscious of the role of the unconscious more than a generation before Freud began to influence modern psychology. Again, exploration of the meaning of the meaning of law was attempted by Holmes half a century before C. K. Ogden and I. A. Richards wrote *The Meaning of Meaning* (1927).

These pioneer contributions, however, though they had organic unity, were made in seemingly disconnected and fugitive writings. An invitation to deliver a series of lectures at the Lowell Institute in Boston happily led him to systematize his ideas into "a connected treatise" and in 1881, before he had crossed forty—a goal he had fiercely set for himself—he published *The Common Law*. The book marks an epoch for law and learning. Together with half a dozen of his essays, *The Common Law* gave the most powerful direction to legal science. The way in which he conceived law and its judicial development was out of the current of the period. He reoriented legal inquiry. The book is a classic in the sense that its stock of ideas has been absorbed and become part of common juristic thought. A few of its opening sentences will give its drift. They represent the thought of today more truly than the temper of the time in which they were written. More than sixty years ago they placed law in a perspective which legal scholarship ever since has merely confirmed. "The life of the law has not been logic: it has been experience. The felt necessities of the time, the prevalent moral and political theories, intuitions of public policy, avowed or unconscious, even the prejudices which judges share with their fellow-men, have had a good deal more to do than the syllogism in determining the rules by which men should be governed. The law embodies the story of a nation's development through many centuries, and it cannot be dealt with as if it contained only the axioms and corollaries of a book of mathematics. In order to know what it is, we must know what it has been, and what it tends to become. We must alternately consult history and existing theories of legislation. But the most difficult labor will be to understand the combination of the two into new products at every stage. The substance of the law at any given time pretty nearly corresponds, so far as it goes, with what is then understood to be convenient; but its form and machinery, and the degree to which it is able to work out desired results, depend very much upon its past."

A work of such seminal scholarship as *The Common Law* makes its way only slowly in affecting the mode of thought of practitioners and judges; but it achieved prompt recognition from the learned world. Its immediate result was a call to Holmes from the Harvard Law School. Largely through the efforts of Louis D. Brandeis, as secretary of the then recently organized Harvard Law

School Alumni Association, a new chair was established for him, and in January 1882, he became Weld Professor of Law, accepting the position with the explicit understanding that he was free to accept a judgeship, should it come his way. On Dec. 5, 1882, Governor John D. Long appointed him to the supreme judicial court of Massachusetts and on Jan. 3, 1883, Holmes took his seat as an associate justice on that bench. This, he used to say, was "a stroke of lightning which changed all the course of my life." Why did Holmes leave the chair for the bench? His aims were never for external power—always his striving was only for "the secret isolated joy of the thinker, who knows that, a hundred years after he is dead and forgotten, men who never heard of him will be moving to the measure of his thought . . ." (*Speeches*, pp. 24–25). But the Civil War evidently influenced him permanently against sheltered thinking. "To think under fire" was his test of most responsible thought. "It is one thing to utter a happy phrase from a protected cloister; another to think under fire—to think for action upon which great interests depend" ("George Otis Shattuck," *Speeches*, p. 73).

While at the bar, on June 17, 1872, he married Fanny Bowditch Dixwell, eldest daughter of his Latin school headmaster, Epes Sargent Dixwell, and grand-daughter of Nathaniel Bowditch, the mathematician. Without some reference to her influence in the Justice's life no sufficiently discerning biography of him is possible. We get an early glimpse of her in several letters from William James. "I have made the acquaintance of . . . Miss (Fanny) Dixwell of Cambridge, lately. She is about as fine as they make 'em. That villain Wendell Holmes has been keeping her all to himself at Cambridge for the last eight years; but I hope I may enjoy her acquaintance now. She is A1, if anyone ever was" (R.B. Perry, *The Thought and Character of William James*, 1935, I, 228; see also *The Letters of William James*, 1920, I, 76, II, 156). One who knew both well for much of their lives, and respected the reserves of both, wrote: "Her quick and vivid perception, her keen wit and vigorous judgment, and the originality and charm of her character cannot be forgotten by anyone who knew her. It is impossible to think of Justice Holmes without thinking of her also. Her effect on his life and career can neither be omitted nor measured in any account of him" (A. D. Hill, in *Harvard Graduates' Magazine*, March 1931, p. 268). She "was in many ways," according to another, "as extraordinary a personality as the Justice himself." She died on Apr. 30, 1929, and to Pollock he wrote: "We have had our share. For sixty years she made life poetry for me . . ." (*Letters*, II, 243).

The stream of litigation that flowed through such an important tribunal as the supreme judicial court of Massachusetts during the twenty years of his incumbency enabled Holmes to fertilize the whole vast field of law. Although questions came before him in the unpremeditated order of litigation, his Massachusetts opinions—nearly 1300—would, if appropriately brought together, constitute the most comprehensive and philosophic body of American law for any period of its history. Except for a synoptic table of his opinions (*Harvard Law Review*,

March 1931, pp. 799–819) and a small selection from them (H. C. Shriver, *The Judicial Opinions of Oliver Wendell Holmes*, 1940), they remain scattered in fifty forbidding volumes of law reports. For him they had the painful inadequacy of one whose aim was the unattainable. "I look into my book in which I keep a docket of the decisions of the full court which fall to me to write, and find about a thousand cases. A thousand cases, many of them upon trifling or transitory matters, to represent nearly half a lifetime! A thousand cases, when one would have liked to study to the bottom and to say his say on every question which the law has ever presented, and then to go on and invent new problems which should be the test of doctrine, and then to generalize it all and write it in continuous, logical, philosophic exposition, setting forth the whole corpus with its roots in history and its justifications of expedience real or supposed" (*Collected Legal Papers*, p. 245).

Such standards were doubtless stimulating to a bar, but were hardly calculated to leave it at ease in Zion. We have a trustworthy view of him as he appeared to lawyers who came before him in Massachusetts: "Nobody who sat on this Court in my time had quite such a daunting personality,—to a young lawyer at least. He was entirely courteous, but his mind was so extraordinarily quick and incisive, he was such an alert and sharply attentive listener, his questions went so to the root of the case, that it was rather an ordeal to appear before him. In arguing a case you felt that when your sentence was half done he had seen the end of it, and before the argument was a third finished that he had seen the whole course of reasoning and was wondering whether it was sound" (unpublished remarks of United States Circuit Judge James M. Morton, Jr., at the exercises in memory of Mr. Justice Holmes before the supreme judicial court of Massachusetts, Oct. 9, 1937). He hated long-windedness and recommended to the gentlemen of the bar the reading of French novels to cultivate the art of innuendo. He expressed himself, however, with sufficient explicitness in some labor cases to be deemed "dangerous" in important circles in Boston. Such was the direction of thought at the time that a dissenting opinion which has since established itself as a great landmark in legal analysis on both sides of the Atlantic (*Vegelahn* vs. *Guntner*, 167 *Mass.*, 92, 104) was seriously felt to be a bar to his judicial promotion. He had simply adhered to his detached view of the law and refused to translate fear of "socialism" "into doctrines that had no proper place in the Constitution or the common law" (*Collected Legal Papers*, p. 295).

He did become chief justice of Massachusetts, on Aug. 5, 1899; and the very opinions which disturbed the conservatism of Boston were in part the influences that led President Theodore Roosevelt to look in Holmes's direction when the resignation of Mr. Justice Horace Gray created a vacancy on the Supreme Bench. Gray was from Massachusetts, and it was natural to turn to Massachusetts for a successor. But the circumstances of Holmes's appointment illustrate what fortuitous elements determine Supreme Court choices. The near approach of the end of Justice Gray's service had been foreshadowed before President McKinley's assasination, and the nomination of Alfred Hemenway, a leading Boston lawyer and partner of McKinley's secretary of the navy, John D. Long, had been decided upon by McKinley. Before it could be made, Theodore Roosevelt had become President and "he did not feel himself bound by the informal arrangement which his predecessor had made with Mr. Hemenway" (unpublished remarks of Judge M. Morton, Jr., *supra*). Roosevelt hesitated not a little about appointing Holmes. A letter to Senator Henry Cabot Lodge gives a full disclosure of Roosevelt's mind on the subject (*Selections from the Correspondence of Theodore Roosevelt and Henry Cabot Lodge*, 1925, I, 517–19). Holmes himself, to a friend, wrote of the curious doubt that troubled Roosevelt, as well as the circumstance that soon stirred his disappointment in Holmes: ". . . he was uneasy about appointing me because he thought I didn't appreciate Marshall. I thought it rather comic. I have no doubt that later he heartily repented over his choice when I didn't do what he wanted in the Northern Securities Case [*Northern Securities Co.* vs. *United States*, 193 *U.S.*, 197]. . . . Long afterwards, at a dinner at the White House to some labor leaders, I said to one of them who had been spouting about the Judges: What you want is favor—not justice. But when I am on my job I don't care a damn what you want or what Mr. Roosevelt wants—and then repeated my remarks to him. You may think that a trifle crude—but I didn't like to say it behind his back and not to his face, and the fact had justified it—I thought and think" (unpublished letter, dated Apr. 1, 1928).

Oliver Wendell Holmes, 1841–1935

Holmes took his seat on Dec. 8, 1902. He came to the Court at a time when vigorous legislative activity reflected changing social conceptions, which in turn were stimulated by vast technological development. What was in the air is well epitomized by the observation that Theodore Roosevelt "was the first President of the United States who openly proposed to use the powers of political government for the purpose of affecting the distribution of wealth in the interest of the golden mean" (C. A. and Mary R. Beard, *The Rise of American Civilization,* 1927, II, 597).

Though formally the product of ordinary lawsuits, constitutional law differs profoundly from ordinary law. For constitutional law is the body of doctrines by which the Supreme Court marks the boundaries between national and state action and by means of which it mediates between citizen and government. The Court thus exercises functions that determine vital arrangements in the government of the American people. These adjustments are based, for the most part, on very broad provisions of the Constitution. Words like "liberty" and phrases like "due process of law" and "regulate commerce . . . among the several States," furnish the text for judgment upon the validity of governmental action directed toward the infinite variety of social and economic facts. But these are words and phrases of "convenient vagueness." They unavoidably give wide judicial latitude in determining the undefined and ever-shifting boundaries between state and nation, between freedom and authority. Even as to these broad provisions of the Constitution distinctions must be observed. In a federated nation, especially one as vast in its territory and varied in its interests as the United States, the power must be somewhere to make the necessary accommodation between the central government and the states. "I do not think the United States would come to an end," said Mr. Justice Holmes, "if we lost our power to declare an Act of Congress void. I do think the Union would be imperilled if we could not make that declaration as to the laws of the several states. For one in my place sees how often a local policy prevails with those who are not trained to national views and how often action is taken that embodies what the Commerce Clause was meant to end" (*Collected Legal Papers*, pp. 295–296). The agency, moreover, must be one not subject to the vicissitudes and pressures under which the political branches of government rest. The Supreme Court is that ultimate arbiter.

Two major issues affecting the whole scheme of government have been the dominant concern of the Supreme Court throughout its history. The Court has had to decide in the most variegated situations from what lawmaking the states are excluded and what legislative domain Congress may enter. And as to both state and national authority it rests with the Court to determine under what circumstances society may intervene and when the individual is to be left unrestricted. But while the Supreme Court thus moves in the perilous sphere of government it does not itself carry the burdens of governing. The Court is merely the brake on other men's actions. Determination of policy—what taxes to impose, how to regulate business, when to restrict freedom—rests with legislatures and executives. The nature of the Court's task thus raises a crucial problem in our constitutional system in that its successful working calls for rare intellectual detachment and penetration, lest limitations in personal experience are transmuted into limitations of the Constitution.

His profound analysis of the sources of our law before he became a judge left in Holmes an abiding awareness of the limited validity of legal principles. He never forgot that circumstances had shaped the law in the past, and that the shaping of future law is primarily the business of legislatures. He was therefore keenly sensitive to the subtle forces that are involved in the process of reviewing the judgment of others not as to its wisdom but as to the reasonableness of their belief in its wisdom. As society became more and more complicated and individual experience correspondingly narrower, tolerance and humility in passing judgment on the experience and beliefs expressed by those entrusted with the duty of legislating, emerge as the decisive factors in constitutional adjudication. No judge could be more aware than Holmes of these subtle aspects of the business of deciding constitutional cases. He read omnivorously to "multiply my scepticisms" (unpublished letter). His imagination and humility, rigorously cultivated, enabled him to transcend the narrowness of his immediate experience. Probably no man who ever sat on the Court was by temperament and discipline freer from emotional commitments compelling him to translate his own economic or social views into constitutional commands. He did not read merely his own mind to discover the powers that may be exercised by a

Holmes, in his estimate of John Marshall, should have subordinated the intellectual originality of the Chief Justice to his political significance. It was to be expected, therefore, that on the Supreme Court he would be left unimpressed by what are called great cases. What he cared about was transforming thought. "My keenest interest is excited, not by what are called great questions and great cases, but by little decisions which the common run of selectors would pass by because they did not deal with the Constitution or a telephone company, yet which have in them the germ of some wider theory, and therefore of some profound interstitial change in the very tissue of the law" (*Collected Legal Papers*, p. 269). Judged by conventional standards, therefore, his opinions not infrequently appeared to dispose rather cavalierly of controversies that were complicated in their facts and far-reaching in their immediate consequences. "This brief summary of the pleadings" he wrote of a litigation in which the record filled a five-foot shelf, "is enough to show the gravity and importance of the case. It concerns the expenditure of great sums and the welfare of millions of men. But cost and importance, while they add to the solemnity of our duty, do not increase the difficulty of decision except as they induce argument upon matters that with less mighty interests no one would venture to dispute" (*Sanitary District* vs. *United States*, *266 U.S.*, 405, 425). With his vast learning he combined extraordinary rapidity of decision. His opinions were felicitous distillates of these faculties. His genius—put to service by rigorous self-discipline and deep learning—was to go for his dissents is less than one per cent of all his opinions. On the Supreme Court of the United States the expression of dissenting views on constitutional issues has, from the beginning, been deemed almost obligatory. In Washington, therefore, they came from Justice Holmes's pen more frequently and sometimes were written with "cold Puritan passion." He gave a public hint of the forces that clashed in the Supreme Court in the decorous form of a mere lawsuit when he said "we are very quiet there, but it is the quiet of a storm centre . . ." (*Collected Legal Papers*, p. 292). In a letter to Pollock he gave more than a hint of the inevitable conflicts within the Court: "To-day I am stirred about a case that I can't mention yet to which I have sent round a dissent that was prepared to be ready as soon as the opinion was circulated. I feel sure that the majority will very highly disapprove of my saying what I think, but as yet it seems to me my duty. No doubt I shall hear about it on Saturday at our conference and perhaps be persuaded to shut up, but I don't expect it" (*Letters*, II, 29). Some of his weightiest utterances are dissents, but they are dissents that have shaped history. (See *Adair* vs. *United States*, 208 *U. S.*, 161, 190; *Hammer* vs. *Dagenhart*, 247 *U. S.*, 251, 277; *Abrams* vs. *United States*, 250 *U. S.*, 616, 624; *Evans* vs. *Gore*, 253 *U. S.*, 245, 264; *Adkins* vs. *Children's Hospital*, 261 *U. S.*, 525, 567; *Tyson* & *Bro.* vs. *Banton*, 273 *U. S.*, 418, 445; *United States* vs. *Schwimmer*, 279 *U. S.*, 644, 653; *Baldwin* vs. *Missouri*, 281 *U. S.* 586, 595.) Disproportionate significance has been attached to his dissents, however; they are merely a part of a much larger, organic whole.

After his retirement he played briefly with the suggestion that he put his ultimate thoughts on law between the covers of a small book, but all his life he had been driven by the lash of some duty undone and at last he revelled in the joy of having no unfinished business. Moreover, he felt strongly that he had had his say in the way in which he most cared to express his reflections—scattered in his more than two thousand opinions and in his lean but weighty collection of occasional writings. "I am being happily idle," he wrote to Pollock, "and persuading myself that 91 has outlived duty. I can imagine a book on the law, getting rid of all talk of duties and rights—beginning with the definition of law in the lawyer's sense as a statement of the circumstances in which the public force will be brought to bear upon a man through the Courts, and expounding rights as a hypostasis of a prophecy—in short, systematizing some of my old chestnuts. But I don't mean to do it . . ." (*Letters*, II, 307). He was no believer in systems. These, he felt, were heavy elaborations of a few insights—*aperçus*, to use his recurring word. Systems die; insights remain, he reiterated. Therefore, a few of his own *aperçus* will give the best clues to his philosophy of law and to his judicial technique in the most important field of his labors.

". . . the provisions of the Constitution are not mathematical formulas having their essence in their form; they are organic living institutions transplanted from English soil. Their significance is vital not formal; it is to be gathered not simply by taking the words and a dictionary, but by considering their origin and the line of their growth" (*Gompers* vs. *United States*, 233 *U. S.*, 604, 610).

"... when we are dealing with words that also are a constituent act, like the Constitution of the United States, we must realize that they have called into life a being the development of which could not have been foreseen completely by the most gifted of its begetters. It was enough for them to realize or to hope that they had created an organism; it has taken a century and has cost their successors much sweat and blood to prove that they created a nation. The case before us must be considered in the light of our whole experience and not merely in that of what was said a hundred years ago" (*Missouri* vs. *Holland*, 252 *U. S.*, 416, 433).

"Great constitutional provisions must be administered with caution. Some play must be allowed for the joints of the machine, and it must be remembered that legislatures are ultimate guardians of the liberties and welfare of the people in quite as great a degree as the courts" (*Missouri, Kansas* & *Texas Ry. Co.* vs. *May*, 194 *U. S.*, 267, 270).

"While the courts must exercise a judgment of their own, it by no means is true that every law is void which may seem to the judges who pass upon it excessive, unsuited to its ostensible end, or based upon conceptions of morality with which they disagree. Considerable latitude must be allowed for differences of view as well as for possible peculiar conditions which this court can know but imperfectly, if at all. Otherwise a constitution, instead of embodying only relatively fundamental rules of whatever combination of native disposition and outside influences it came to pass, however, the result was that Holmes early rejected legal principles as absolutes. He looked beneath their decorous formulations and saw them for what they usually are—sententious expressions of overlapping or conflicting social policies. The vital judicial issue is apt, therefore, to be their accommodation. Decisions thus become essentially a matter of drawing lines. Again and again he adverted to that necessity, which he once summed up as follows: "I do not think we need trouble ourselves with the thought that my view depends upon differences of degree. The whole law does so as soon as it is civilized. . . . Negligence is all degree—that of the defendant here degree of the nicest sort; and between the variations according to distance that I suppose to exist and the simple universality of the rules in the Twelve Tables or the Leges Barbarorum, there lies the culture of two thousand years" (*LeRoy Fibre Co.* vs. *Chicago, Milwaukee* & *St. Paul Ry.*, 232 *U. S.*, 340, 354). Such a view of law of course implies the exercise of choice. But judicial judgment precluded the notion of capricious choice. It assumes judgment between defined claims, each of recognized validity and with a cultural pedigree of its own, but all of which necessarily cannot be completely satisfied. This process of adjustment is bound increasingly to fall to the legislature as interests and activities in society become more and more interdependent. The considerations which thus prompt legislation and the intricate, dubious materials out of which laws are written bring into sharp focus the duty of deference to legislative determinations demanded from the revisory process called adjudicative. In a thousand instances Holmes was loyal to that philosophy. Thereby he resolved into comprehending larger truths the conflicting claims of state and nation, of liberty and authority, of individual and society.

"It is right and proper that in the reading room of the Harvard Law School the portrait of Holmes should face in equal honor the portrait of Marshall" (A. D. Hill, *Harvard Graduates' Magazine, supra,* p. 284). There fell to Marshall, as Holmes took occasion to say, "perhaps the greatest place that ever was filled by a judge" (*Collected Legal Papers,* p. 270). That Marshall seized it, the role of the Supreme Court in American history bears witness. Holmes's claim to preeminence has a different basis. He is unsurpassed in the depth of his penetration into the nature of the judicial process and in the originality of its exposition. His conception of the Constitution cannot be severed from his conception of a judge's function in applying it; and his views of the judge's function derive from his intellectual presuppositions, that is, from his loyal adherence in judicial practice to his philosophic scepticism. His approach to judicial problems was inseparable from his consciously wrought notions of his relations to the universe. These abstractions appear far removed from the particular cases that came before him. But the clarity with which a specific controversy is seen, in the context of the larger intellectual issues beneath the formal surface of litigation, and the disinterestedness with which such analysis guides decision and opinion, are the ultimate determinants of American public law.

After a major operation in the summer of 1922,

Holmes showed signs of age—he was then in his eighty-second year; but his marvelous physique gradually reasserted itself, though he strictly conserved his energy for his work. Some of his most powerful opinions were written in his ninth decade. Until near the end of his tenure he usually wrote more than his share of opinions. He was nearly eighty-nine when the illness and death of Chief Justice Taft cast upon Holmes for a considerable period the heavy burden of presiding in Court and the still more difficult task of guiding its deliberations at conferences. He did both, in the language of Mr. Justice Brandeis, "as to the manner born."

The machinery was running down, however, and on Jan. 12, 1932, he sent his resignation, in his own beautiful script, to the President—"the time has come and I bow to the inevitable." He continued his serene life, in Washington and in the summers at Beverly Farms, reading and being read to, enjoying the simple and familiar things of nature that had always refreshed him and the devoted attention of friends, especially the young. He had become a very old man but his faculties were never impaired. He had grown almost wistful in his gentleness. The fire of his exciting personality was dying down and on the morning of Mar. 6, 1935, came the end.

With the sure response of the mass of men—given enough time—to goodness and gallantry of spirit, Holmes, the fundamentally solitary thinker, had become a pervasive and intimate national possession. His death elicited an outpouring of feeling throughout the country. But of all the moving things that were said he would probably have most liked the few words of his old friend and his closest colleague for fifteen years, Mr. Justice Brandeis, when the news was brought him: "And so the great man is gone." On his ninety-fourth birthday—a raw March day with snow gently falling—he was buried with due military honors, in the Arlington National Cemetery, alongside his wife and near his companions, known and unknown, of the Army of the Potomac.

Without accompanying explanation, he left the bulk of his substantial estate to the nation, the largest unrestricted gift ever made to it. Congress established a Holmes Fund Memorial Commission, whose proposals, interrupted by the Second World War, await the consideration of Congress.* In a message to that body recommending an appropriate use of the bequest, President Franklin Roosevelt thus interpreted Holmes's intention: "It is the gift of one who, in war and in peace, devoted his life to its [his country's] service. Clearly he thereby sought, with a generous emphasis, to mark the full measure of his faith in those principles of freedom which the country was founded to preserve." And the President expressed what he deemed to be the country's desire that Congress "translate this gift into a form that may serve as a permanent impulse for the maintenance of the deepest tradition that Mr. Justice Holmes embodied." That tradition, wrote President Roosevelt, "was a faith in the creative possibilities of the law. For him law was an in-

* By an act of Congress approved on August 5, 1955, a Permanent Committee for the Oliver Wendell Holmes Devise was created, to supervise the preparation and publication of a history of the Supreme Court, and, in its discretion, to support an annual lecture or series of lectures and a memorial volume containing selections from the writings of Mr. Justice Holmes.

strument of just relations between man and man. With an insight into its history that no American scholar has surpassed; with a capacity to mold ancient principles to present needs, unique in range and remarkable in prophetic power; with a grasp of its significance as the basis upon which the purposes of men are shaped, Mr. Justice Holmes sought to make the jurisprudence of the United States fulfill the great ends our nation was established to accomplish" (President's Message to Congress, Apr. 25, 1935).

[Holmes's Massachusetts opinions may be found in *Mass. Reports*, vols. 134–82; for analytical table see *Harvard Law Rev.*, Mar. 1931, for chronological, H. C. Shriver, *Judicial Opinions of Oliver Wendell Holmes* (1940). His Supreme Court opinions are in *U. S. Reports*, vols. 187–284, and an analytical table is in *Harvard Law Rev., supra.* Alfred Lief, *Dissenting Opinions of Mr. Justice Holmes* (1929) and *Representative Opinions of Mr. Justice Holmes* (1931) give selections. For bibliog. of early writings and selections see *Harvard Law Rev., supra;* these and others are reprinted in Shriver, *Justice Oliver Wendell Holmes: His Book Notices and Uncollected Letters and Papers* (1936). *The Common Law* (1881, 1938) has been translated into several foreign languages. His *Speeches* (1891), with additions, was reprinted in 1913 and 1938. H. J. Laski, ed., *Collected Legal Papers* (1920) contains speeches and essays. Only two full series of his correspondence have thus far been published—M. DeW. Howe, *Holmes-Pollock Letters* (2 vols., 1941) and letters to J. C. H. Wu, published in *T'ien Hsia Monthly*, Oct. 1935, and reprinted in Shriver, *Book Notices*.* R. B.

* Collections that have appeared since the first publication of this essay include *Touched with Fire: Civil War Letter and Diary of Oliver Wendell Holmes, Jr., 1861–1864* (1946), ed. by M. DeW.

Perry, *The Thought and Character of William James* (1935) contains correspondence between James and Holmes. Other collections are in the Lib. of Cong., the Harvard Law School Lib., and private possession. Critical and biog. material may be found in *Mr. Justice Holmes, a Collection of Essays* (1931), ed. by Felix Frankfurter; Silas Bent, *Justice Oliver Wendell Holmes* (1932); Felix Frankfurter, *Mr. Justice Holmes and the Supreme Court* (1939); Francis Biddle, *Mr. Justice Holmes* (1942); Max Lerner, *The Mind and Faith of Justice Holmes* (1943); Catherine D. Bowen, *Yankee from Olympus* (1943).]

Howe; "The Holmes-Cohen Correspondence," *Journal of the History of Ideas*, IX, 3–52 (January 1948), ed. by Felix S. Cohen; and *Holmes-Laski Letters: The Correspondence of Mr. Justice Holmes and Harold J. Laski* (2 vols., 1953), ed. by M. DeW. Howe.

Mr. Justice Holmes and the Supreme Court

NOTE

The following lectures were delivered to the general public on April 11, 18, and 25, 1938, as part of the program of the Committee on Extracurricular Reading in American History of Harvard University. They are now published at the request of the sponsors of these lectures. To recast them would mean the writing of another kind of book. I have, therefore, retained the original form of the lectures, which, as written, were intended for laymen.

It is a pleasurable duty to acknowledge my indebtedness to Mr. Adrian S. Fisher, Research Fellow of the Harvard Law School, for his assistance in their preparation.

Appendices are added, setting forth in detail the range of invalidation of state legislation through the Fourteenth Amendment. The drudgery of compiling these materials was generously assumed by Messrs. William Du B. Sheldon, Edward F. Prichard, Jr., and Adrian S. Fisher.*

F. F.

1 June, 1938
Cambridge, Massachusetts

* These Appendices are omitted in this edition.

Introductory

THE HISTORY of the Supreme Court would record fewer explosive periods if, from the beginning, there had been a more continuous awareness of the rôle of the Court in the dynamic process of American society. Lawyers, with rare exceptions, have failed to lay bare that the law of the Supreme Court is enmeshed in the country's history; historians no less have seemed to miss the fact that the country's history is enmeshed in the law of the Supreme Court. Normally historians, much more than lawyers, guide the general understanding of our institutions. But historians have, in the main, allowed only the most spectacular decisions—the Dred Scott controversy or the Legal Tender Cases—to intrude upon the flow of national development through their voluminous pages. The vital share of the Court in the interplay of the country's political and economic forces has largely escaped their attention. Not unnaturally the Court has been outside the permanent focus of the historian's eye. For the momentum of the Court's influence has been achieved undramatically and imperceptibly, like the gradual growth of a coral reef, as the cumulative product of hundreds of cases, individually unexciting and seemingly even unimportant, but in their total effect powerfully telling in the pulls and pressures of society. And so the rather arid doctrines of lawyers have largely held the field. This has had two unfortunate aspects. The public has been denied understanding of the intimate share of the Supreme Court in the affairs of States and Nation; the Supreme Court has been deprived of that healthy play of informed criticism from without which is indispensable for the vitality of every institution.

The technical forms in which issues come before the Court and the professional atmosphere which dominates opinions have helped to build up the tradition of the Court as a body quite dissociated from the conflicts of politics. To be sure, some business of the Court is of a strictly technical nature. These matters are important, of course; but, on the whole, they are limited in their scope to the interests of the immediate litigants and others similarly circumstanced. Lawyers call it, properly enough, private litigation. But of this there was much more before the Court one hundred years ago than fifty years ago, more fifty years ago than twenty-five years ago, and today it might fairly be characterized as a minor aspect of the activities of the Court.[1] Such litigation—that is, ordinary controversies between Jones and Smith

[1] Felix Frankfurter and J. M. Landis, *The Business of the Supreme Court* (New York, 1928), p. 302.

—would never have made the Court the storm center of politics it has sometimes become. It is the Court's public business that has excited public interest.

From the very beginning the Court has had business which in form was an ordinary lawsuit but which affected the nation as much as action either by the Congress or by the President. The raw material of modern government is business. Taxation, utility regulation, agricultural control, labor relations, housing, banking and finance, control of the security market—all our major domestic issues—are phases of a single central problem, namely, the interplay of economic enterprise and government. These are the issues which for more than a generation have dominated the calendar of the Court. For the special function of the Supreme Court in our scheme of things is to mediate between the individual and government, and to mark the boundaries between state and national action. The Court is the final authority in adjusting the relationships of the individual to the separate states, of the individual to the United States, of the forty-eight states to one another, and of the states to the Union.

The Supreme Court exercises this tremendous authority as interpreter of clauses of the Constitution. But the clauses which are interpreted differ drastically in their nature and history, and therefore present sharply different problems for interpretation. Broadly speaking, there are two types of constitutional clauses. First are specific provisions designed to guard against the recurrence of well-defined historic grievances or to impose some specific limitation of power either upon the states or the central government in the distribution of authority under our federalism. These provisions are so definite in their terms and in their history that they canalize interpretation within narrow limits. For that reason they are seldom brought into question and even more rarely excite conflicting views about their meaning. Whether a "fact tried by a jury" has been "re-examined in any Court of the United States" otherwise than "according to the rules of the common law," whether a crime is "infamous," whether a tax is laid upon articles exported from any state, even whether the prohibition against "unreasonable searches and seizures" has been violated, allow comparatively meager play for individual judgment as to policy; they are neither frequent nor fighting issues before the Court.

In the second category are the broad, undefined clauses of the Constitution setting out standards of fair dealing, as well as doctrines of government not expressed in the Constitution but derived from assumptions regarding its purposes. These clauses and implicit doctrines of the Constitution bring very different problems to the Court from those just indicated. Words like "liberty" and "property," phrases like "regulate Commerce . . . among the several States," "due process of law," "equal protection of the laws," doctrines like those of the separation of powers and the non-delegability of the legislative function, are the foundation for judicial action upon the whole appalling domain of social and economic fact. But phrases like "due process of law" are, as an able judge once expressed it, of "convenient vagueness."[2] Their am-

[2] C. M. Hough, "Due Process of Law—To-day," *Harvard Law Review*, XXXII (January 1919), 218.

biguity is such that the Court is compelled to put meaning into the Constitution, not to take it out. Such features of the Constitution render peculiarly appropriate a favorite quotation of John Chipman Gray: "Whoever hath an absolute authority to interpret any written or spoken law, it is he who is truly the lawgiver to all intents and purposes, and not the person who first wrote or spoke them."[3] Thus, in deciding whether an act of Congress is a deprivation of property or a Massachusetts tax is an undue burden on interstate commerce, the scope for interpreting the Constitution is relatively wide and the opportunity for exercising individual notions of policy correspondingly free. This is the most active and controversial sphere of Supreme Court litigation. Within it the justices are cartographers who give temporary location but do not ultimately define the evershifting boundaries between state and national power, between freedom and authority.

It is plain, therefore, that judges are not merely expert reporters of pre-existing law. Because of the free play of judgment allowed by the Constitution, judges inevitably fashion law. And law is one of the shaping forces of society. That is why to neglect the Supreme Court's role in our social and economic history is to omit vital factors of the story. The Supreme Court gives direction to economic forces, especially to the pace and the range of their incidence. No matter how powerful the pressures behind the use of the corporation as an instrument of enterprise, it cannot be denied that the Supreme Court has enor-

[3] From a sermon by Bishop Hoadley, quoted in Gray, *The Nature and Sources of the Law* (2nd ed., New York, 1921), pp. 102, 125, 172.

mously furthered corporate growth. By devising facilities for business conducted through the corporate form and protecting it from policies hostile or inhospitable to corporate enterprise, the decisions of the Court themselves have operated as economic factors.

We speak of the Court as though it were an abstraction. To be sure, the Court is an institution, but individuals, with all their diversities of endowment, experience and outlook, determine its actions. The history of the Supreme Court is not the history of an abstraction, but the analysis of individuals acting as a Court who make decisions and lay down doctrines, and of other individuals, their successors, who refine, modify, and sometimes even overrule the decisions of their predecessors, reinterpreting and transmuting their doctrines. In law, also, men make a difference. It would deny all meaning to history to believe that the course of events would have been the same if Thomas Jefferson had had the naming of Spencer Roane to the place to which John Adams called John Marshall, or if Roscoe Conkling rather than Morrison R. Waite had headed the Court before which came the Granger legislation. The evolution of finance capital in the United States, and therefore of American history after the Reconstruction period, would hardly have been the same if the views of men like Mr. Justice Miller and Mr. Justice Harlan had dominated the decisions of the Court from the Civil War to Theodore Roosevelt's administration. There is no inevitability in history except as men make it.

are treacherous, except in so far as a man's genius breaks through a collective judgment, or his vivid life before he went on the bench serves as commentary, or as he expresses individual views in dissent or through personal writings. Not to speak of the present Court, Mr. Justice Holmes possessed these qualities of personal genius perhaps in richer measure than any member in the Court's history.

The Chief Justice of Massachusetts became Mr. Justice Holmes of the Supreme Court on December 4, 1902, and resigned on January 12, 1932. He was thus a member of the Court for more than a fifth of its entire active history, and participated in more than a third of its adjudications. More important than these items of duration or volume is the historic significance of the period. Long-maturing social forces which the Civil War released or intensified found powerful political expression just about the time that Mr. Justice Holmes went to Washington. Time did not abate these conflicts. And so it came about that the Court, during his whole thirty years, was sucked into political controversies more continuous and of more immediate popular concern than at any time in its history.

To the discerning, the burst of capitalistic activity following the victory of the North early revealed that reconciliation of unfettered individual enterprise with social well-being would be the chief issue of politics. A letter by Mr. Justice Miller, written in 1878, which has recently come to light, is a straw showing the way the wind was blowing. Miller, an appointee of Lincoln and probably the most powerful member of his Court, kept a close watch on events in Washington as well as from the vantage point of the agricultural Middle West, where he traveled much on circuit:

> I have met with but few things of a character affecting the public good of the whole country that has shaken my faith in human nature as much as the united, vigorous, and selfish effort of the capitalists,—the class of men who as a distinct class are but recently known in this country—I mean those who live solely by interest and dividends. Prior to the late war they were not numerous. They had no interest separate from the balance of the community, because they could lend their money safely and at high rates of interest. But one of the effects of the war was greatly to reduce the rate of interest by reason of the great increase in the quantity of the circulating medium. Another was by the creation of a national funded debt, exempt from taxation, to provide a means for the investment of surplus capital. This resource for investment was quadrupled by the bonds issued by the States, by municipal corporations, and by Rail Road companies. The result has been the gradual formation of [a] new kind of wealth in this country, the income of which is the coupons of interest and stock dividends, and of a class whose only interest or stake in the country is the ownership of these bonds and stocks. They engage in no commerce, no trade, no manufacture, no agriculture. *They produce nothing.*[1]

Mr. Justice Miller was here describing early manifestations of the impact of technological science upon society. Finance capital was in its early stages. Its evolution since Mr. Justice Miller wrote has been analyzed in Veblen's

[1] Charles Fairman, "Justice Samuel F. Miller—A Study of a Judicial Statesman," *Political Science Quarterly*, L (March 1935), 15, 21.

writings and in Brandeis' *Other People's Money;* the pungent details are recorded in the massive volumes of the Pecora investigating committees. In brief, technological advances led to large-scale industry, large-scale industries flowered into mergers and monopolies, thereby producing in considerable measure a subordination of industry to finance. On the social side came the shift from a dominantly agricultural to an urbanized society. Big business stimulated modern trade unionism. Since modern politics is largely economics, these conflicting forces soon found political expression. After several abortive attempts, the various agrarian and progressive movements, in combination with organized labor and other less defined groups, three times won the presidency. For the "square deal" of Theodore Roosevelt, the "new freedom" of Woodrow Wilson, and the "new deal" of Franklin D. Roosevelt have a common genealogy. Disregarding for the moment detailed or minor differences, the three eras which these slogans summarize derived from efforts to reconcile modern economic forces with the demands of a popular democracy.

The result of the process of economic concentration in the half century since the Miller letter is luminously conveyed by some Treasury figures. I quote from Solicitor General Robert H. Jackson in his recent report on the Sherman Law:

> In 1932, according to the statistics of the Bureau of Internal Revenue, 53 percent of all corporate owned assets in this country was held by 618 corporations, which constitutes only 0.2 of 1 percent of the number of corporations reporting. Five percent of the corporations owned 85 percent

of all corporate owned wealth in 1932. More than 50 percent of all the net income enjoyed by corporations in 1932 went to 232 corporations, while of the country's manufacturing corporations 1.2 percent of the total number accounted for 63 percent of the aggregate net profits. In 1934 the only group of corporations to earn an aggregate net profit was the group whose assets exceeded $50,000,000. Thus, the process of concentration was continuing.

There was likewise a high degree of concentration in the ownership of these corporations. 1929 was a banner year for stock ownership and in that year the 3.28 percent of the population who filed individual income tax returns accounted for the receipt of more than 83 percent of all dividends paid to individuals. And 78 percent of those dividends reported were received by 0.3 of 1 percent of our population.

The effect of this centralization is reflected in the distribution of national income. In 1933 the Bureau of Internal Revenue statistics show that there were only 1,747,740 taxable individual incomes in the United States and nearly one-third of all the property reported as passing by death was found in less than 4 percent of the estates. Brookings Institution's studies of 1929 show that about 6,000,000 families, or 21 percent of all families, had family incomes of less than $1,000 annually, and that 36,000 families in the high income brackets received as much of our national income in that year as 11,000,000 families with the lowest income.[2]

Instead of using dry figures Mr. Bernard Baruch, who is uniquely equipped to describe it, has portrayed the present economic scene by a few swift strokes:

"In the industrial east, at least, individual intiative had begun to merge into corporate collectivism" around the end of the 19th century, attaining its fullest effect in the decade

[2] *Report of the Attorney General for the Fiscal Year 1937*, p. 36.

following the world war. It has long since replaced "the older capitalism" as the dominant force in our economic life. Naturally, there is only one means of controlling this collectivist growth in corporate enterprise. Government regulation must be extended to a direct proportionate degree. This is a sine qua non which business must accept.[3]

Short of the immediate issues of today, Mr. Justice Holmes' period of service on the Court covered the years of most intense interaction between government and business. Barring the tariff and the National Bank Act there were only two important measures of economic legislation on the federal statute books when Mr. Justice Holmes came to the Court, and these two, the Interstate Commerce Act of 1887 and the Sherman Law of 1890, had only somnolent vitality. Nor had state legislation, after the flurry of the Granger days, proved itself an effective device for social control over economic circumstance. Theodore Roosevelt's presidency marked the change. Under him the federal government for the first time embarked upon a positive program of social welfare. Through use of the taxing power and by regulatory legislation, not only were abuses to be remedied but benefits to be achieved for the common man. A vast field of hitherto free enterprise was brought under governmental supervision. Regardless of the political complexion of successive administrations, the area of national oversight of business was extended. From 1903 to 1932, an invigorated Interstate Commerce Commission, the Federal Trade Commission, the Federal Reserve Board,

[3] Letter in *Springfield Republican*, Saturday, March 26, 1938, p. 6.

the Farm Loan Board, the Tariff Commission, the Federal Power Commission, the Railroad Labor Board, followed each other in quick succession.

This vigorous legislative movement was partly a reflex of energetic state action and partly stimulated states to action. Wisconsin, under the elder La Follette, and New York, under Charles E. Hughes, took the lead in effective state regulation of utilities. In the decade between 1910 and 1920 all but half a dozen states enacted workmen's compensation laws. Local anti-trust laws, shorter hours acts, minimum wage laws, blue-sky laws, banking laws, conservation enactments, illustrate only some of the topics on which laws came from the forty-eight states for eventual judgment by Mr. Justice Holmes' Court.

In this response of legislation to the new world created by modern industry, the United States was merely repeating British experience. The American story of agitation, investigation, and legislation is registered in the well-known British blue books, containing reports of royal commissions on modern economic and industrial problems, as they have manifested themselves in Great Britain and throughout the British Dominions. This struggle between the individualistic habits of the early nineteenth century and legislation as a means of effectuating the common interest is familiar to every reader of Dicey's brilliant *Law and Opinion in England*.

Such were the problems, however embedded in legal forms and phrased in legal jargon, that came to Mr. Justice Holmes for adjudication.

What equipment did he bring to the Court for dealing

with these problems? What qualities did President Theodore Roosevelt look for, in appointing a Supreme Court justice at this time? Most things are kept from us that touch the intimate history of the Court, and so we are seldom allowed to share the private thoughts of a President on the considerations which moved him in making a Supreme Court appointment. Thanks to Senator Lodge, the elder, to whom President Roosevelt unburdened his mind, we do know both the hopes and the doubts that he felt about Mr. Justice Holmes' qualifications for the Supreme Bench, at that particular time:

First of all, I wish to go over the reasons why I am in his favor. . . . The labor decisions which have been criticized by some of the big railroad men and other members of large corporations, constitute to my mind a strong point in Judge Holmes' favor. The ablest lawyers and the greatest judges are men whose past has naturally brought them into close relationship with the wealthiest and most powerful clients, and I am glad when I can find a judge who has been able to preserve his aloofness of mind so as to keep his broad humanity of feeling and his sympathy for the class from which he has not drawn his clients. I think it eminently desirable that our Supreme Court should show in unmistakable fashion their entire sympathy with all proper effort to secure the most favorable possible consideration for the men who most need that consideration.

Now a word as to the other side. . . . In the ordinary and low sense which we attach to the words "partisan" and "politician," a judge of the Supreme Court should be neither. But in the higher sense, in the proper sense, he is not in my judgment fitted for the position unless he is a party man, a constructive statesman, constantly keeping in mind his adherence to the principles and policies under which this nation has been built up and in accordance with which it must go on; and keeping in mind also his relations with his fellow statesmen who in other branches of the government are striving in cooperation with him to advance the ends of government. . . .

. . . The majority of the present Court who have, although without satisfactory unanimity, upheld the policies of President McKinley and the Republican party in Congress, have rendered a great service to mankind and to this nation. The minority—a minority so large as to lack but one vote of being a majority—have stood for such reactionary folly as would have hampered well-nigh hopelessly this people in doing efficient and honorable work for the national welfare. . . .

Now I should like to know that Judge Holmes was in entire sympathy with our views, that is with your views and mine . . . before I would feel justified in appointing him. Judge Gray has been one of the most valuable members of the Court. I should hold myself as guilty of an irreparable wrong to the nation if I should put in his place any man who was not absolutely sane and sound on the great national policies for which we stand in public life.[4]

In taking account of the general philosophy of a prospective member of the Supreme Court towards major public issues likely to come before it, Theodore Roosevelt was merely following the example of other presidents, notably Lincoln in appointing Chase as Chief Justice. The psychological assumptions made by Theodore Roosevelt and Lincoln that the past in which a man is inured may have a powerful effect upon his future decisions are supported by weighty judicial experience. In

[4] *Selections from the Correspondence of Theodore Roosevelt and Henry Cabot Lodge*, I (New York, 1925), 517–19.

the intimacy of family correspondence, Mr. Justice Miller has given us a glimpse of the personal influences which shape impersonal legal opinions:

> It is vain to contend with judges who have been at the bar the advocates for forty years of railroad companies, and all the forms of associated capital, when they are called upon to decide cases where such interests are in contest. All their training, all their feelings are from the start in favor of those who need no such influence.[5]

We have been educated to an awareness of the enormous role which the unconscious plays in ordinary life, and the best of judges are beginning to realize, as Mr. Justice Holmes did long ago, how profoundly important it is that a judge be on his guard lest he read "his conscious or unconscious sympathy with one side or the other prematurely into the law." When judges decide issues that touch the nerve center of economic and social conflict, the danger, in de Tocqueville's phrase, of confounding the familiar with the necessary is especially hazardous. The matter was put with candor by Lord Justice Scrutton, a great English judge:

> The habits you are trained in, the people with whom you mix, lead to your having a certain class of ideas of such a nature that, when you have to deal with other ideas, you do not give as sound and accurate a judgment as you would wish. This is one of the great difficulties at present with Labour. Labour says: "Where are your impartial Judges? They all move in the same circle as the employers, and they are all educated and nursed in the same ideas as the employers. How can a labour man or a trade unionist get impartial

[5] Fairman, in *Political Science Quarterly*, L, 43, n. 4.

justice?" It is very difficult sometimes to be sure that you have put yourself into a thoroughly impartial position between two disputants, one of your own class and one not of your class.[6]

Unlike the great men on the Court before him, Mr. Justice Holmes had been singularly outside the current of public affairs or of interest in them. He was essentially the philosopher who turned to law. Ultimate issues of the destiny of man, not the evanescent events of the day, preoccupied his mind. That he did not read newspapers revealed neither affectation nor a sense of superiority; it mirrored his worldly innocence. When Senator Lodge tried to induce him to run for governor, with the bait that it would inevitably lead to a seat in the United States Senate, Mr. Justice Holmes blandly replied: "But I don't give a damn about being Senator." And yet, though he did not bring to the Court the experience of great affairs, not even Marshall exceeded him in judicial statesmanship. Other great judges have been guided by the wisdom distilled from an active life; Mr. Justice Holmes was led by the divination of the philosopher and the imagination of the poet.

Because he had an organic philosophy, he was not distracted by the infinite diversity of detail in the appearance of the same central issues. No one realized better than he that, while principles gain significance through application, concrete instances are inert except when galvanized into life by a general principle. And so it is per-

[6] Scrutton, "The Work of the Commercial Courts," *Cambridge Law Journal*, I (1921), 6, 8.

haps more true of him than of any other judge in the history of the Court that the host of public controversies in which he participated was subdued to reason by relatively few guiding considerations. This was true whether he was called upon to strike a balance between the claims of property and its obligations, or between the rights of individuals and their duties, or between the limits of state action and the authority of the federal government.

Indeed, underlying all the myriad forms of these great problems is an antecedent issue. What is the role of a judge in making these adjustments between society and the individual, between the states and the nation? The conception which a judge has of his own function, and the fastidiousness with which he follows it, will in large measure determine the most delicate controversies before him. Justices of the Court are not architects of policy. They can nullify the policy of others; they are incapable of fashioning their own solutions for social problems. The use which a judge makes of this power of negation is largely determined by two psychological considerations. It depends first on the judge's philosophy, conscious or implicit, regarding the nature of society; that is, on his theory of the clash of interests. This, in turn, will influence his conception of the place of the judge in the American constitutional system.

Mr. Justice Holmes' view of the play of forces in society hardly differed from that of Madison in his classic statement in the *Federalist:*

> Those who hold and those who are without property have ever formed distinct interests in society. Those who are

creditors, and those who are debtors, fall under a like discrimination. A landed interest, a manufacturing interest, a mercantile interest, a moneyed interest, with many lesser interests, grow up of necessity in civilized nations, and divide them into different classes, actuated by different sentiments and views. The regulation of these various and interfering interests forms the principal task of modern legislation, and involves the spirit of party and faction in the necessary and ordinary operations of the government.[7]

Thirty years before he went on the Supreme Court, Mr. Justice Holmes expressed this view in his own way:

This tacit assumption of the solidarity of the interests of society is very common, but seems to us to be false . . . in the last resort a man rightly prefers his own interest to that of his neighbors. And this is as true in legislation as in any other form of corporate action. All that can be expected from modern improvements is that legislation should easily and quickly, yet not too quickly, modify itself in accordance with the will of the *de facto* supreme power in the community, and that the spread of an educated sympathy should reduce the sacrifice of minorities to a minimum. . . . The objection to class legislation is not that it favors a class, but either that it fails to benefit the legislators, or that it is dangerous to them because a competing class has gained in power, or that it transcends the limits of self-preference which are imposed by sympathy. . . . But it is no sufficient condemnation of legislation that it favors one class at the expense of another; for much or all legislation does that; and none the less when the *bona fide* object is the greatest good of the greatest number . . . if the welfare of all future ages is to be considered, legislation may as well be abandoned for the present. . . . The fact is that legislation in this country,

[7] *The Federalist,* No. 10 (sesquicentennial ed., Washington, 1937), p. 56.

as well as elsewhere, is empirical. It is necessarily made a means by which a body, having the power, put burdens which are disagreeable to them on the shoulders of somebody else.[8]

Mr. Justice Holmes never forgot that the activities of government are continual attempts by peaceful means to adjust these clashes of interest, and he was equally mindful of the fact that the body to whom this task of adjustment is primarily delegated is the legislature. And so he gave complete loyalty in his work as a judge to the major premise of Marshall "that it is a *Constitution* we are expounding."[9] He scrupulously treated the Constitution as a broad charter of powers for the internal clashes of society, and did not construe it as though it were a code which prescribed in detail answers for the social problems of all time.

Thus, the enduring contribution of Mr. Justice Holmes to American history is his constitutional philosophy. He gave it momentum by the magic with which he expressed it. Great judges are apt to be identified with what lawyers call great cases. The achievements of his great predecessors have, on the whole, to be recounted through an analysis of specific decisions, their meaning and their consequences. Mr. Justice Holmes' specialty was great utterance. He dealt with intrinsic significance, not with meretricious, because evanescent, importance. "Great cases," he himself has said, "are called great, not

[8] Holmes, "The Gas-Stokers' Strike," *American Law Review,* VII (1873), 583, reprinted in *Harvard Law Review,* XLIV (March 1931), 795.

[9] McCulloch v. Maryland, 4 Wheat. 316, 407 (U.S. 1819).

by reason of their real importance in shaping the law of the future, but because of some accident of immediate, overwhelming interest which appeals to the feelings and distorts the judgment." He saw the vital in the undramatic; to him, inconspicuous controversies revealed the clash of great social forces. And so the significance of his genius would evaporate in any analysis of specific decisions. In his case, form and substance were beautifully fused. His conception of the Constitution must become part of the political habits of the country, if our constitutional system is to endure; and if we care for our literary treasures, the expression of his views must become part of our national culture.

The Constitution is, of course, a legal document, but a legal document of a fundamentally different order than an insurance policy or a lease of timberland. For the Justice, the Constitution was not primarily a text for dialectic but a means of ordering the life of a progressive people. While its roots were in the past, it was projected for the unknown future:

. . . the provisions of the Constitution are not mathematical formulas having their essence in their form; they are organic living institutions transplanted from English soil. Their significance is vital not formal; it is to be gathered not simply by taking the words and a dictionary, but by considering their origin and the line of their growth.[10]

. . . when we are dealing with words that also are a constituent act, like the Constitution of the United States, we must realize that they have called into life a being the development of which could not have been foreseen completely

[10] Gompers v. United States, 233 U.S. 604, 610 (1914).

by the most gifted of its begetters. It was enough for them to realize or to hope that they had created an organism; it has taken a century and has cost their successors much sweat and blood to prove that they created a nation. The case before us must be considered in the light of our whole experience and not merely in that of what was said a hundred years ago.[11]

While the Supreme Court is thus in the exacting realm of government, it is itself freed from the terrible burdens of governing. The Court is the brake on other men's actions, the judge of other men's decisions. Responsibility for action rests with legislators. The range of the Court's authority is thus very limited, but its exercise may vitally affect the nation. No wonder John Marshall spoke of this power of the Court as "delicate."[12]

No man who ever sat on the Court has been more keenly or more consistently sensitive than Mr. Justice Holmes to the dangers and difficulties inherent in the power of judges to review legislation. For it is subtle business to decide, not whether legislation is wise, but whether legislators were reasonable in believing it to be wise. In view of the complexities of modern society and the restricted scope of any man's experience, tolerance and humility in passing judgment on the worth of the experience and beliefs of others become crucial faculties in the disposition of cases. The successful exercise of such judicial power calls for rare intellectual disinterestedness and penetration, lest limitation in personal experience and imagination operate as limitations of the Constitution.

[11] Missouri v. Holland, 252 U.S. 416, 433 (1920).
[12] Fletcher v. Peck, 6 Cranch 87, 128 (U.S. 1810).

These insights Mr. Justice Holmes applied in hundreds of cases and expressed in memorable language:

> It is a misfortune if a judge reads his conscious or unconscious sympathy with one side or the other prematurely into the law, and forgets that what seem to him to be first principles are believed by half his fellow men to be wrong. . . . When twenty years ago a vague terror went over the earth and the word socialism began to be heard, I thought and still think that fear was translated into doctrines that had no proper place in the Constitution or the common law.[13]
>
> While the courts must exercise a judgment of their own, it by no means is true that every law is void which may seem to the judges who pass upon it excessive, unsuited to its ostensible end, or based upon conceptions of morality with which they disagree. Considerable latitude must be allowed for differences of view as well as for possible peculiar conditions which this court can know but imperfectly, if at all. Otherwise a constitution, instead of embodying only relatively fundamental rules of right, as generally understood by all English-speaking communities, would become the partisan of a particular set of ethical or economical opinions, which by no means are held *semper ubique et ab omnibus*.[14]

If these had been merely the views of a closet philosopher they would not have aroused dissent, nor would they have been seriously noticed. But when they were made the effective instruments of adjudication they became fighting issues. By cutting beneath the surface of decisions Mr. Justice Holmes exposed their psychological and sociological roots. While in the eighties and nineties our economy was in process of drastic transformation,

[13] Holmes, *Collected Legal Papers* (New York, 1920), p. 295.
[14] Otis v. Parker, 187 U.S. 606, 608–09 (1903).

members of the Supreme Court continued to reflect the economic order in which they grew up. Between the presidencies of Grant and the first Roosevelt, *laissez faire* was the dominant economic social philosophy, and it was imported into the Constitution. Temporary facts were translated into legal absolutes; abstract conceptions concerning "liberty of contract" were erected into constitutional dogmas. Malleable and undefined provisions of the Constitution were applied as barriers against piecemeal efforts of adjustment through legislation to a society permeated by the influence of technology, large-scale industry, progressive urbanization, and the general dependence of the individual on economic forces beyond his control. The due process clauses were especially the destructive rocks on which this legislation foundered. Judge Learned Hand, one of the most eminent of our judges, has said that the requirement of due process is merely an embodiment of the English sporting idea of fair play. In England, particularly from the time of the Campbell-Bannerman government, the same causes that induced American legislative attempts led to a continual Parliamentary modification of the system of private enterprise. The scope of this trend in England is revealed by a few tell-tale figures. The social services established by this legislation have entailed an increase in expenditure from 19*s.* 2*d.* per capita in 1900 to £8 16*s.* 6*d.* in 1934; and about a third of the national income of Great Britain is now spent through public channels.[15]

Yet as late as 1905 the Supreme Court held it uncon-

[15] Frankfurter, "Foreword," *Yale Law Journal*, XLVII (1938), 515, 516.

stitutional to limit the working hours of bakers to ten,[16] and as recently as 1936 the Court adhered to its ruling that it was beyond the power both of the states and of the nation to assure minimum wage rates for women workers obviously incapable of economic self-protection.[17] Every variety of legislative manifestation to subject economic power to social responsibility encountered the judicial veto.

The doctrinal process by which the majority reached such results was thus explained by Mr. Justice Holmes in dissenting from his brethren in the Minimum Wage case:

> . . . The only objection that can be urged [against a minimum wage law for women for the District of Columbia] is found within the vague contours of the Fifth Amendment, prohibiting the depriving any person of liberty or property without due process of law. To that I turn.
>
> The earlier decisions upon the same words in the Fourteenth Amendment began within our memory and went no farther than an unpretentious assertion of the liberty to follow the ordinary callings. Later that innocuous generality was expanded into the dogma, Liberty of Contract. Contract is not specially mentioned in the text that we have to construe. It is merely an example of doing what you want to do, embodied in the word liberty. But pretty much all law consists in forbidding men to do some things that they want to do, and contract is no more exempt from law than other acts.[18]

The practical meaning of this operation of judicial review was put by the late Judge Hough with characteristic pungency: "No man has seen more plainly that the

[16] Lochner v. New York, 198 U.S. 45 (1905).
[17] Morehead v. New York *ex rel.* Tipaldo, 298 U.S. 587 (1936).
[18] Adkins v. Children's Hospital, 261 U.S. 525, 568 (1923).

court was measuring the legislature's reasons by its own intellectual yardstick than has Justice Holmes; none more keenly perceived that the notations thereupon marked those results of environment and education which many men seem to regard as the will of God or the decrees of fate."[19] Against this subtle danger of the unconscious identification of personal views with constitutional sanction Mr. Justice Holmes battled during all his years on the Court. For a short time after the bake-shop case his views were in the ascendant. Chief Justice White was heard to attribute to the influence exerted by President Theodore Roosevelt no inconsiderable share in the shift of the Court's emphasis. The fact is that for less than a decade, between 1908 and the World War, the Court did allow legislation to prevail which, in various aspects, regulated enterprise with reference to its social consequences and withdrew phases of industrial relations from the area of illusory individual bargaining.[20]

But those who had assumed a permanent change in the Court's outlook were soon disappointed. Changes in the Court's personnel and in the general economic and social climate of the Harding-Coolidge era soon reflected themselves in decisions. Until after the 1936 election, the Court was back to the high tide of judicial negation reached in the Lochner case, in 1905. Mr. Justice Holmes' classic dissent in that case will never lose its relevance:

> This case is decided upon an economic theory which a large part of the country does not entertain. If it were a

[19] Hough, in *Harvard Law Review*, XXXII, 232, n. 2.

[20] *E.g.*, Muller v. Oregon, 208 U.S. 412 (1908); Bunting v. Oregon, 243 U.S. 426 (1917).

question whether I agreed with that theory, I should desire to study it further and long before making up my mind. But I do not conceive that to be my duty, because I strongly believe that my agreement or disagreement has nothing to do with the right of a majority to embody their opinions in law. It is settled by various decisions of this court that state constitutions and state laws may regulate life in many ways which we as legislators might think as injudicious or if you like as tyrannical as this, and which equally with this interfere with the liberty to contract. Sunday laws and usury laws are ancient examples. A more modern one is the prohibition of lotteries. The liberty of the citizen to do as he likes so long as he does not interfere with the liberty of others to do the same, which has been a shibboleth for some well-known writers, is interfered with by school laws, by the Post Office, by every state or municipal institution which takes his money for purposes thought desirable, whether he likes it or not. The Fourteenth Amendment does not enact Mr. Herbert Spencer's Social Statics. . . . Some of these laws embody convictions or prejudices which judges are likely to share. Some may not. But a constitution is not intended to embody a particular economic theory, whether of paternalism and the organic relation of the citizen to the State or of *laissez faire*. It is made for people of fundamentally differing views, and the accident of our finding certain opinions natural and familiar or novel and even shocking ought not to conclude our judgment upon the question whether statutes embodying them conflict with the Constitution of the United States.[21]

This was the great theme of his judicial life—the amplitude of the Constitution as against the narrowness of some of its interpreters. And so, having analyzed with brave clarity the governing elements in the modern economic struggle, he did not shrink from giving his analysis

[21] 198 U.S. 45, 75–76 (1905).

judicial recognition. "One of the eternal conflicts out of which life is made up," he wrote, more than forty years ago, "is that between the effort of every man to get the most he can for his services, and that of society, disguised under the name of capital, to get his services for the least possible return. Combination on the one side is patent and powerful. Combination on the other is the necessary and desirable counterpart, if the battle is to be carried on in a fair and equal way."[22] Mr. Justice Holmes therefore found nothing in the Constitution to prevent legislation which sought to remove some of the more obvious inequalities in the distribution of economic power.

Economists and historians are now largely agreed that the resistance to a natural and responsible trade unionism has been one of the most disturbing factors in our economy. Had the views of Mr. Justice Holmes prevailed, the Constitution would not have been used as an obstruction to the healthy development of trade unionism. More than thirty years ago he protested when a majority of the Court invalidated an act of Congress against the "yellow dog" contract which, as a matter of history, was drawn by Richard Olney and sponsored by President Cleveland. The need for legislation to remove disabilities against the effective right of association by workers became more manifest with time. State after state, therefore, passed laws to assure trade unions the opportunity which they already had in the rest of the English-speaking world. But a majority of the Court remained obdurate and imposed a doctrinaire view of the Constitution against such legis-

[22] Vegelahn v. Guntner, 167 Mass. 92, 108 (1896).

lation.[23] One can only surmise what would have been the gain to social peace and economic security had the dissenting views expressed more than twenty years ago by Mr. Justice Holmes been the Court's views:

In present conditions a workman not unnaturally may believe that only by belonging to a union can he secure a contract that shall be fair to him. . . . If that belief, whether right or wrong, may be held by a reasonable man, it seems to me that it may be enforced by law in order to establish the equality of position between the parties in which liberty of contract begins. Whether in the long run it is wise for the workingmen to enact legislation of this sort is not my concern, but I am strongly of opinion that there is nothing in the Constitution of the United States to prevent it. . . .[24]

Law, he was well aware, not merely confirms property interests; it helps to create them. The availability of legal remedies may itself be a potent instrument of economic power. Correspondingly, the withholding of such remedies may affect the balance of conflicting interest in the economic struggle. Mr. Justice Holmes denied that the Constitution stereotyped any particular distribution of economic power for all time. With the clean precision of a surgeon he uncovered the process by which, under the guise of deductive reasoning, partial claims were given the shelter of the Constitution as comprehensive interests of property:

Delusive exactness is a source of fallacy throughout the law. By calling a business "property" you make it seem like

[23] Adair v. United States, 208 U.S. 161 (1908).
[24] Coppage v. Kansas, 236 U.S. 1, 26–27 (1915).

land, and lead up to the conclusion that a statute cannot substantially cut down the advantage of ownership existing before the statute was passed. An established business no doubt may have pecuniary value and commonly is protected by law against various unjustified injuries. But you cannot give it definiteness of contour by calling it a thing. It is a course of conduct and like other conduct is subject to substantial modification according to time and circumstances both in itself and in regard to what shall justify doing it a harm.[25]

By a steady extension of doctrines which, to Mr. Justice Holmes, had no justification in the Constitution, a majority of the Court persistently denied exertions of the legislature toward reconciling individual enterprise and social welfare. Abstract conceptions regarding property and "liberty of contract" were the swords with which these measures were struck down. Mr. Justice Holmes was finally roused to an unusual judicial protest. His dissent from the decision of the majority in declaring unconstitutional a New York statute regulating theatre-ticket scalping fully reveals his mind. It also gives a glimpse of the importance he attached to art throughout life:

We fear to grant power and are unwilling to recognize it when it exists . . . when legislatures are held to be authorized to do anything considerably affecting public welfare it is covered by apologetic phrases like the police power, or the statement that the business concerned has been dedicated to a public use. The former expression is convenient, to be sure, to conciliate the mind to something that needs explanation: the fact that the constitutional requirement of compensation

[25] Truax v. Corrigan, 257 U.S. 312, 342–43 (1921).

when property is taken cannot be pressed to its grammatical extreme; that property rights may be taken for public purposes without pay if you do not take too much; that some play must be allowed to the joints if the machine is to work. But police power often is used in a wide sense to cover and, as I said, to apologize for the general power of the legislature to make a part of the community uncomfortable by a change.

I do not believe in such apologies. I think the proper course is to recognize that a state legislature can do whatever it sees fit to do unless it is restrained by some express prohibition in the Constitution of the United States or of the State, and that Courts should be careful not to extend such prohibitions beyond their obvious meaning by reading into them conceptions of public policy that the particular Court may happen to entertain. Coming down to the case before us I think, as I intimated in *Adkins* v. *Children's Hospital*, 261 U. S. 525, 569, that the notion that a business is clothed with a public interest and has been devoted to a public use is little more than a fiction intended to beautify what is disagreeable to the sufferers. The truth seems to me to be that, subject to compensation when compensation is due, the legislature may forbid or restrict any business when it has a sufficient force of public opinion behind it. Lotteries were thought useful adjuncts of the State a century or so ago; now they are believed to be immoral and they have been stopped. Wine has been thought good for man from the time of the Apostles until recent years. But when public opinion changed it did not need the Eighteenth Amendment, notwithstanding the Fourteenth, to enable a State to say that the business should end. *Mugler* v. *Kansas*, 123 U. S. 623. What has happened to lotteries and wine might happen to theatres in some moral storm of the future, not because theatres were devoted to a public use, but because people had come to think that way.

But if we are to yield to fashionable conventions, it seems

to me that theatres are as much devoted to public use as anything well can be. We have not that respect for art that is one of the glories of France. But to many people the superfluous is the necessary, and it seems to me that Government does not go beyond its sphere in attempting to make life livable for them. I am far from saying that I think this particular law a wise and rational provision. That is not my affair. But if the people of the State of New York speaking by their authorized voice say that they want it, I see nothing in the Constitution of the United States to prevent their having their will.[26]

Taxation is perhaps the severest testing ground for the objectivity and wisdom of a social thinker. The enormous increase in the cost of society and the extent to which wealth is now represented by intangibles, the profound change in the relation of the individual to government and the resulting widespread insistence on security, are subjecting public finance to the most exacting demands. To balance budgets, to pay for the costs of progressively civilized social standards, to safeguard the future and to divide these burdens fairly among different interests in the community, put the utmost strain on the ingenuity of statesmen. They must constantly explore new sources of revenue and find means of preventing the circumvention of their discoveries. Subject as they are, in English-speaking countries, to popular control, they should not be denied adequate latitude of power for their extraordinarily difficult tasks.

Mr. Justice Holmes never yielded to finicky limitations or doctrinaire formulas, drawn from the general language

[26] Tyson & Bro. v. Banton, 273 U.S. 418, 445–47 (1927).

of the Constitution, as a means of circumscribing the discretion of legislatures in the necessarily empirical process of tapping new revenue or stopping new devices for its evasion. He did not have a curmudgeon's feelings about his own taxes. A secretary who exclaimed, "Don't you hate to pay taxes!" was rebuked with the hot response, "No, young feller. I like to pay taxes. With them I buy civilization." And as a judge he consistently refused to accentuate fiscal difficulties of government by injecting into the Constitution his own notions of fiscal policy. Nor did he believe that there was anything in the Constitution to bar even a conscious use of the taxing power for readjusting the social equilibrium. One of his last utterances gives the general flavor of his many opinions in tax cases:

I have not yet adequately expressed the more than anxiety that I feel at the ever increasing scope given to the Fourteenth Amendment in cutting down what I believe to be the constitutional rights of the States. As the decisions now stand, I see hardly any limit but the sky to the invalidating of those rights if they happen to strike a majority of this Court as for any reason undesirable. I cannot believe that the Amendment was intended to give us *carte blanche* to embody our economic or moral beliefs in its prohibitions. Yet I can think of no narrower reason that seems to me to justify the present and the earlier decisions to which I have referred. . . . It seems to me to be exceeding our powers to declare such a tax a denial of due process of law.

And what are the grounds? Simply, so far as I can see, that it is disagreeable to a bondholder to be taxed in two places. Very probably it might be good policy to restrict taxation to a single place, and perhaps the technical conceptions of domicil may be the best determinant. But it seems to me that if that result is to be reached it should be reached through understanding among the States, by uniform legislation or otherwise, not by evoking a constitutional prohibition from the void of "due process of law," when logic, tradition and authority have united to declare the right of the State to lay the now prohibited tax.[27]

I have indicated the general direction of Mr. Justice Holmes' judicial mind on the great issues of the constitutional position of property in our society. During most of his thirty years on the Supreme Bench, and especially during the second half of his tenure, his were not the views of a majority of the Court. But the good that men do lives after them. About a year ago the old views of Mr. Justice Holmes began to be the new constitutional direction of the Court.[28] His own constitutional outlook was, throughout a long life, free from fluctuations. This was so because it was born of a deeply rooted and coherent philosophy concerning the dynamic character of the American Constitution and of a judge's function in construing it. If he threw the weight of his authority on the side of social readjustments through legislation it was not because of any faith in panaceas in general or in measures of social amelioration in particular. He personally "disbelieved all the popular conceptions of socialism," and came dangerously close to believing in the simplicities of the wage-fund theory.[29] But his scepticism and even hostility, as a matter of private judgment, toward legislation

[27] Baldwin v. Missouri, 281 U.S. 586, 595–96 (1930).
[28] West Coast Hotel Co. v. Parrish, 300 U.S. 379 (1937).
[29] See Plant v. Woods, 176 Mass. 492, 505 (1900).

which he was ready to sustain as a judge only serve to add cubits to his judicial stature. For he thereby transcended personal predilections and private notions of social policy, and became truly the impersonal voice of the Constitution.

⋘ II ⋙

Civil Liberties and the Individual

WE HAVE seen that the unfolding of the powerful economic forces released after the Civil War furnished the chief grist for constitutional litigation from the time that Mr. Justice Holmes went to Washington. There is truth behind the familiar contrast between rights of property and rights of man. But certainly in some of its aspects property is a function of personality, and conversely the free range of the human spirit becomes shrivelled and constrained under economic dependence. Especially in a civilization like ours where the economic interdependence of society is so pervasive, a sharp division between property rights and human rights largely falsifies reality. A good deal of the history of the United States may fairly be summarized as the process, complicated and confused, of bringing to the masses economic freedom commensurate with their political freedom. But the various interests of human personality are not of equal worth. There is a hierarchy of values. And so we shall find that some manifestations of the human spirit seemed to Mr. Justice Holmes so precious that in specific instances he found no justification for legislative restrictions, tolerant though he was of the legislative judgment. Thus he accorded to some claims the protection of the Constitution which he denied to others, although all claimed the shelter of the "liberty" which it protects.

The Justice deferred so abundantly to legislative judgment on economic policy because he was profoundly aware of the extent to which social arrangements are conditioned by time and circumstances, and of how fragile, in scientific proof, is the ultimate validity of a particular economic adjustment. He knew that there was no authoritative fund of social wisdom to be drawn upon for answers to the perplexities which vast new material resources had brought. And so he was hesitant to oppose his own opinion to the economic views of the legislature. But history had also taught him that, since social development is a process of trial and error, the fullest possible opportunity for the free play of the human mind was an indispensable prerequisite. Since the history of civilization is in considerable measure the displacement of error which once held sway as official truth by beliefs which in turn have yielded to other truths, the liberty of man to search for truth was of a different order than some economic dogma defined as a sacred right because the temporal nature of its origin had been forgotten. And without freedom of expression, liberty of thought is a mockery. Nor can truth be pursued in an atmosphere hostile to the endeavor or under dangers which only heroes hazard.

Naturally, therefore, Mr. Justice Holmes attributed very different legal significance to those liberties of the individual which history has attested as the indispensable conditions of a free society from that which he attached to liberties which derived merely from shifting economic arrangements. These enduring liberties of the subject, in the noble English phrase, were, so far as the national government is concerned, specifically enshrined in the Bill of Rights. But they have gradually found protection even against state action through a slow process of expansion of the liberty secured by the Fourteenth Amendment, after that clause, in the course of half a century, had established itself as the instrument for supervising the whole gamut of state legislation. Because these civil liberties were explicitly safeguarded in the Constitution, or conceived to be basic to any notion of the liberty guaranteed by the Fourteenth Amendment, Mr. Justice Holmes was far more ready to find legislative invasion in this field than in the area of debatable economic reform.

His hardy scepticism did not answer with easy confidence Milton's rhetorical question: "whoever knew Truth put to the worse, in a free and open encounter" with "Falsehood"? In nothing did he have deeper faith than in the free interchange of ideas. Yet he did not erect even freedom of speech into a dogma of absolute validity nor enforce it to doctrinaire limits. In his view, only a timid and debilitated society need fear in the long run the ferment of truth-seeking. Circumstances, however, may obstruct the operation of the long run. The exigencies of time condition the fate of societies. One whose whole outlook on life was profoundly influenced by his

Civil War experience was bound to acquiesce in some subordination of private opinion during war which he would find unwarranted in times of peace.

It fell to him to speak for the Court in first upholding legislation curbing freedom of utterance during the World War. While the incitement to resist war measures even by conscientious pacifists fell foul of the Espionage Acts, Mr. Justice Holmes was careful not to give a loose warrant to the government to curb expression of opinion. At the very outset he laid down cautionary limits against inroads upon freedom of speech not actually embarrassing the nation's safety:

> We admit that in many places and in ordinary times the defendants in saying all that was said in the circular would have been within their constitutional rights. But the character of every act depends upon the circumstances in which it is done. . . . The most stringent protection of free speech would not protect a man in falsely shouting fire in a theatre and causing a panic. . . . The question in every case is whether the words used are used in such circumstances and are of such a nature as to create a clear and present danger that they will bring about the substantive evils that Congress has a right to prevent. It is a question of proximity and degree. When a nation is at war many things that might be said in time of peace are such a hindrance to its effort that their utterance will not be endured so long as men fight and that no Court could regard them as protected by any constitutional right.[1]

War stimulates lawlessness, sometimes even in officers of the law. This was true of England during the Napoleonic wars; it was true of the United States as a result of the World War. Lincoln went to the heart of the problem

[1] Schenck v. United States, 249 U.S. 47, 52 (1919).

in his first message to Congress: "Must a government of necessity be too *strong* for the liberties of its own people, or too *weak to* maintain its own existence?"[2] The extent to which World War legislation was bent to a brutal and lawless spirit is now a matter of history. Referring to the *Report upon the illegal Practices of the United States Department of Justice*,[3] the present Chief Justice, in June 1920, spoke as follows: "Very recently information has been laid by responsible citizens at the bar of public opinion of violations of personal rights which savor of the worst practices of tyranny."[4] And a few years later Mr. Moorfield Storey made this handsome, penitential amende: "On a small scale a 'reign of terror' [was produced] in which some thousands of innocent people were very cruelly treated and exposed to much suffering and loss. . . . The statements in the newspapers were false and misleading. There was no conspiracy to overthrow this government and no evidence was ever produced which excused the action of the government. The safeguards of the Constitution were ignored and any true American must blush at what was done and at the indifference in which he, and all but a handful of his countrymen, tolerated it."[5]

It is necessary to recall those days because they help

[2] J. D. Richardson, ed., *A Compilation of the Messages and Papers of the Presidents*, VI (Washington, 1897), 23.

[3] Washington, 1920.

[4] C. E. Hughes, "Some Observations on Legal Education and Democratic Process," *Two Addresses Delivered before the Alumni of the Harvard Law School* (1920), p. 23.

[5] Louis F. Post, *The Deportations Delirium of Nineteen-Twenty* (Chicago, 1923), p. xii.

to illumine subsequent judicial development. The abuses of this period of hysteria undoubtedly focussed the attention of Mr. Justice Holmes on the practical consequences of a relaxed attitude toward the specific prohibition of the First Amendment of the Constitution: "Congress shall make no law . . . abridging the freedom of speech." He was again in the minority, supported only by Mr. Justice Brandeis, in demanding scrupulous observance of this explicit requirement of the Bill of Rights. It is not reckless prophecy to assume that his famous dissenting opinion in the Abrams case will live as long as English prose retains its power to move:

> I do not doubt for a moment that by the same reasoning that would justify punishing persuasion to murder, the United States constitutionally may punish speech that produces or is intended to produce a clear and imminent danger that it will bring about forthwith certain substantive evils that the United States constitutionally may seek to prevent. The power undoubtedly is greater in time of war than in time of peace because war opens dangers that do not exist at other times.
>
> But as against dangers peculiar to war, as against others, the principle of the right to free speech is always the same. It is only the present danger of immediate evil or an intent to bring it about that warrants Congress in setting a limit to the expression of opinion where private rights are not concerned. Congress certainly cannot forbid all effort to change the mind of the country. . . .
>
> In this case sentences of twenty years' imprisonment have been imposed for the publishing of two leaflets that I believe the defendants had as much right to publish as the Government has to publish the Constitution of the United States now vainly invoked by them. Even if I am technically

wrong and enough can be squeezed from these poor and puny anonymities to turn the color of legal litmus paper; I will add, even if what I think the necessary intent were shown; the most nominal punishment seems to me all that possibly could be inflicted, unless the defendants are to be made to suffer not for what the indictment alleges but for the creed that they avow—a creed that I believe to be the creed of ignorance and immaturity when honestly held, as I see no reason to doubt that it was held here, but which, although made the subject of examination at the trial, no one has a right even to consider in dealing with the charges before the Court.

Persecution for the expression of opinions seems to me perfectly logical. If you have no doubt of your premises or your power and want a certain result with all your heart you naturally express your wishes in law and sweep away all opposition. To allow opposition by speech seems to indicate that you think the speech impotent, as when a man says that he has squared the circle, or that you do not care wholeheartedly for the result, or that you doubt either your power or your premises. But when men have realized that time has upset many fighting faiths, they may come to believe even more than they believe the very foundations of their own conduct that the ultimate good desired is better reached by free trade in ideas—that the best test of truth is the power of the thought to get itself accepted in the competition of the market, and that truth is the only ground upon which their wishes safely can be carried out. That at any rate is the theory of our Constitution. It is an experiment, as all life is an experiment. Every year if not every day we have to wager our salvation upon some prophecy based upon imperfect knowledge. While that experiment is part of our system I think that we should be eternally vigilant against attempts to check the expression of opinions that we loathe and believe to be fraught with death, unless they so imminently threaten immediate interference with the lawful and pressing purposes of the law that an immediate check is required to save the country. I wholly disagree with the argument of the Government that the First Amendment left the common law as to seditious libel in force. History seems to me against the notion. I had conceived that the United States through many years had shown its repentance for the Sedition Act of 1798, by repaying fines that it imposed. Only the emergency that makes it immediately dangerous to leave the correction of evil counsels to time warrants making any exception to the sweeping command, "Congress shall make no law . . . abridging the freedom of speech." Of course I am speaking only of expressions of opinion and exhortations, which were all that were uttered here, but I regret that I cannot put into more impressive words my belief that in their conviction upon this indictment the defendants were deprived of their rights under the Constitution of the United States.[6]

One of the favorite admonitions of the Justice was that we should think things and not words. His own rigorous discipline against confounding personal predispositions with the order of nature largely saved him from letting phrases do service for actuality. His brethren sustained an order of the Postmaster General withdrawing a second class mail permit for an alleged violation of the War Espionage Act by treating postal facilities as a privilege, and, therefore, subject to wide discretion in permitting its enjoyment. With a few strokes of his pen Mr. Justice Holmes brushed away this web of unreality:

The United States may give up the Post Office when it sees fit, but while it carries it on the use of the mails is almost

[6] Abrams v. United States, 250 U.S. 616, 627–28, 629–31 (1919).

as much a part of free speech as the right to use our tongues and it would take very strong language to convince me that Congress ever intended to give such a practically despotic power to any one man.[7]

In his resolute insistence on keeping open the channels of free though heretical inquiry, Mr. Justice Holmes was a traditionalist. He found Constitutional confirmation for the tradition in which he was bred—the tradition of Emerson and Thoreau and Garrison. Hostility to freedom of speech takes protean forms, but Mr. Justice Holmes was alert to discover it in its various disguises. He found it, as we have seen, in the threat of sentences so disproportionate as to create a terrorizing atmosphere. He pierced through the disguise of excessive administrative discretion, and saw it as throttling power, in the circumstances of the day, over the means of disseminating news. Nor would he allow the sovereign authority of the United States over naturalization of aliens to be the means of penalizing unpopular opinion. In serener days a sense of humor would have saved the denial of citizenship to an otherwise estimable woman of forty-nine simply because, as a pacifist, she declined to promise to bear arms for the United States in a future war. Mr. Justice Holmes cut through the agitated atmosphere of the time to the deeper confidence in human reason expressed by the Bill of Rights:

Some of her answers might excite popular prejudice, but if there is any principle of the Constitution that more imperatively calls for attachment than any other it is the prin-

[7] Milwaukee Publishing Co. v. Burleson, 255 U.S. 407, 437 (1921).

ciple of free thought—not free thought for those who agree with us but freedom for the thought that we hate. I think that we should adhere to that principle with regard to admission into, as well as to life within, this country. And recurring to the opinion that bars this applicant's way, I would suggest that the Quakers have done their share to make the country what it is, that many citizens agree with the applicant's belief and that I had not supposed hitherto that we regretted our inability to expel them because they believe more than some of us do in the teachings of the Sermon on the Mount.[8]

The end of the war shifted the major interest in the problem of freedom of speech from national to state concern. Just as the French Revolution hung for nearly a generation over English opinion and led to much repressive legislation, so in the twenties the Russian revolution was a cloud overhanging the American scene. Partly fashion and partly fear led to many state laws against radical propaganda. When these measures came before the Court, they did not have the support of war necessities, but neither was it possible to invoke such a specific constitutional claim as that which the First Amendment affords. So far as the Federal Constitution was concerned, criminal syndicalism laws offended only if the freedom of speech which they curbed was included in the "liberty" of the Fourteenth Amendment. Mr. Justice Holmes found no difficulty in finding here a forbidden legislative interference. Because of the overriding importance which he attached to freedom of discussion, he practically absorbed the specific protection of freedom of speech of the

[8] United States v. Schwimmer, 279 U.S. 644, 654–55 (1929).

First Amendment in the generality of the concept of "liberty" in the Fourteenth. In one case as in the other he would allow the tongue to be fettered only if there was a clear and present danger to the safety of the state when judged by a sturdy fear. For him outlawry of opinion, merely because it was despised, violated one of these "relatively fundamental rules of right, as generally understood by all English-speaking communities" embodied in the Constitution:

> If what I think the correct test is applied, it is manifest that there was no present danger of an attempt to overthrow the government by force on the part of the admittedly small minority who shared the defendant's views. It is said that this manifesto was more than a theory, that it was an incitement. Every idea is an incitement. It offers itself for belief and if believed it is acted on unless some other belief outweighs it or some failure of energy stifles the movement at its birth. The only difference between the expression of an opinion and an incitement in the narrower sense is the speaker's enthusiasm for the result. Eloquence may set fire to reason. But whatever may be thought of the redundant discourse before us it had no chance of starting a present conflagration. If in the long run the beliefs expressed in proletarian dictatorship are destined to be accepted by the dominant forces of the community, the only meaning of free speech is that they should be given their chance and have their way.[9]

These instances must suffice to show the different considerations that determined Mr. Justice Holmes' mind when he sat in judgment on legislation attempting economic readjustments as against legislation restricting freedom of utterance. Just as he would allow experiments in

[9] Gitlow v. New York, 268 U.S. 652, 673 (1925).

economics which he himself viewed with doubt and distrust, so he would protect speech that offended his taste and wisdom. At bottom both attitudes came from a central faith and a governing scepticism. Since the whole of truth has not yet been, and is not likely to be, brought up from its bottomless well, the first duty of an educated man was to doubt his major premise even while he continued to act on it. This was the sceptical conviction with which he distrusted dogma, whether economic or intellectual. But his was never the paralyzing scepticism which easily becomes comfortable or corroding cynicism. He had a positive faith—faith in the gradual power to pierce nature's mysteries through man's indomitable endeavors. This was the road by which he reached an attitude of widest tolerance towards views which were strange and uncongenial to him, lest by a premature stifling even of crude or groping ideas society might be deprived of eventual wisdom for attaining a gracious civilization.

That a majority of the Court which frequently disallowed restraints upon economic power should so consistently have sanctioned restraints of the mind is perhaps only a surface paradox. There is an underlying unity between fear of ample experimentation in economics and fear of expression of heretical ideas. On the other hand, since, in Mr. Justice Holmes' view, action derives from ideas, his belief in the evolutionary process of social institutions committed him to the fullest freedom of the mind.

Not until after his death, indeed not until the other

day, did the powerful seeds of his dissents bear fruit in the decisions of the Court.[10] The new attitude of judicial tolerance towards the endeavors of a democratic society to grapple with the domestic manifestations of world-wide economic difficulties has its counterpart in tolerance towards dissident views, even in opposition to gusts of legislative folly. In these as in all other matters, Mr. Justice Holmes had no exaggerated notions about the role of the Supreme Court. It can do much. But much also depends on local functionaries, on the police and prosecutors, on the skill and the public spirit of the bar. And so whenever opportunity afforded, as in the awful circumstances of Leo Frank's trial[11] and in the dangerous practice of wire tapping—"dirty business," he called it[12] —he gave concrete and eloquent point to his "main remedy" for the ills of society, namely, that we should "grow more civilized." But neither court and counsel nor police and prosecution are the ultimate reliances for the liberties of the people. These rest in ourselves. The liberties that are defined by our Bill of Rights are, on the whole, more living realities in the daily lives of Englishmen without any formal constitution because they are part of the national habit, they are in the marrow of the bones of the people. Such habits become a national tradition through constant renewal in thought and in deed. The literary form in which they are embodied is itself a creative force for achieving that end. What Mr. Justice

[10] Herndon v. Lowry, 301 U.S. 242 (1937).
[11] Frank v. Magnum, 237 U.S. 309, 345 (1915).
[12] Olmstead v. United States, 277 U.S. 438, 470 (1928).

Holmes did during his thirty years on the Supreme Court to vindicate the claims of Anglo-American liberty through law has not been exceeded by the achievement of any judge. But by the manner of his doing it he has wrought even more greatly, in that he has added to the golden treasury of the nation's spiritual heritage.

«III»

The Federal System

THE ECONOMIC revolution caused by technology, combined with the influence of Darwinism on man's way of thinking about his destiny, has, in every democratic society, enormously intensified the problem of reconciling property rights with human rights and has vastly complicated the great issue of freedom and social obligation. These conundrums of government are rendered still more elusive and harassing for us and our statesmen because they must be solved within the recondite legal arrangements of our federalism.

Limiting ourselves to English-speaking rule, it is no mere accident that such vast regions as the United States, Canada, Australia, and India are federal, and not unitary, states. History explains much. All these nations were unions of hitherto separate governments. But South Africa also was a union, and a union of rather obstreperous parts. Yet South Africa is not a truly federated so-

so the basis of these English-speaking federalisms—of all federalism, indeed—is a written constitution. The explicit language of these documents has made certain division of power between central and local governments so clear as to leave no room for conflict short of rebellion. But in other areas of government disputes are bound to give rise to controversies of interpretation. Some tribunal must adjust these controversies. We find, therefore, in all English-speaking federalisms a court for settling these inevitable clashes, in so far as law can settle them.

That different circumstances give rise to variations in the distribution of power between a national government and its constituents is amply illustrated by the conditions attending the formation of the three English federalisms —Canada in 1867, Australia in 1900, and the Federation of India in 1935. Canada was framing her organic act while the United States was rent by Civil War. The experience Canadians drew from the conflict was the weakness of the American system due to excessive authority in the states. And so Canada largely reversed the American scheme by restricting the provinces to defined powers and leaving the residuum of control to the Dominion. Thirty years later Australia was more concerned to maintain the autonomy of her states; she therefore based her scheme of division between state and commonwealth authority on the eighteenth-century American Constitution. India presented her own distinctive complexities, because of the vastness of the population with their social and religious differences, and the tantalizing adjustments that have to be made to bring the provinces and the Princes' states within the same federation. As a result, the

Government of India Act, 1935, formulates a plan of exclusive federal powers, exclusive provincial powers, and concurrent powers, much more complicated than that provided for any other English-speaking country.

In these conspicuous instances, the momentum of federalism has proved stronger than the centripetal forces of modern society. Despite the powerful economic unifications due to the revolution in technology, federalism continues to be the form of political union. Judicial application of some clauses of the Australian Constitution had given rise to fret and friction. This led Australia, twenty-five years after federation, to charge a Royal Commision with examining "the working" of its Constitution. That Commission, in 1929, reported adherence to the essentials of the federal scheme. In Canada there is now sitting a distinguished Royal Commission on Dominion-Provincial Relations, but no one expects it to recommend a transformation of Canadian federalism into a unitary state. And the various hopes for self-government in India express themselves within the conception of a federated society.

Federal governments are not the offspring of political science; they are the product of economic and social pressures. Such was the origin of our Union. The government that preceded the United States was a collaborative arrangement of thirteen states that had won their independence. But it is much easier to win independence than to work it. In pursuit of legal sovereignty, they were in danger of losing the substance of the well-being for which society exists. Independence became self-destructive. In the classic analysis of Madison, some of the states "having no convenient ports for foreign commerce, were subject to be taxed by their neighbors, through whose ports their commerce was carried on. New Jersey, placed between Philadelphia and New York, was likened to a cask tapped at both ends; and North Carolina, between Virginia and South Carolina, to a patient bleeding at both arms."[1] The practical inadequacies of the Articles of Confederation largely determined the means for their correction.

What were the dominating inadequacies? First, such national government as there was had to come hat in hand to the states. It was dependent upon their voluntary subordination of shortsighted state interests to the common good. The national government had no authority to enforce the national will directly upon individuals. They were not citizens of the nation but only citizens of Massachusetts or New York or Virginia. Secondly, the mercantilism pursued by the thirteen states was in effect a policy of economic feud which Balkanized an area dependent on the free interchange of goods. Their triumph over these powerful disintegrating forces was the great achievement of the framers of the Constitution. The result was the establishment of a central government supreme in its sphere, with power to protect the economic interests common to all the states and to enforce its authority directly upon the people, not merely by grace of the states.

The terms embodying the authority for the three

[1] See Max Farrand, *The Framing of the Constitution* (New Haven, 1913), p. 7.

charters of government for the union of our states, are symbolic. "We, the undersigned Delegates of the States," was the description of the source of the Articles of the Confederation. The seceding states took even more pains to underline state autonomy when, in framing the Constitution of the Confederate States, they wrote, "We the people of the Confederate States, each State acting in its sovereign and independent character." By contrast, "We, the people of the United States," as the formula for the source of the Constitution may have been merely of literary origin, but it is one of those happy accidents of phrasing to which historical development has given psychological significance.

As a matter of text, the history of the Constitution has been one of permanence. Its changes have been few, and these have not seriously affected the structure of our government. The Eleventh Amendment, protecting the states against unpermitted suits by individuals, only reinstated the view generally held when the Constitution was adopted. The Sixteenth Amendment did confer upon the national government power of immense practical significance, in enabling it to levy income taxes without apportionment according to population. This amendment merely restored a power which the federal government had exercised from time to time for a hundred years, but which, by the narrowest margin, the Supreme Court, in 1895, in the much criticized Income Tax Cases,[2] unexpectedly denied to the nation. The Eighteenth Amend-

[2] Pollock v. Farmers' Loan & Trust Co., 157 U.S. 429 (1895); s.c. 158 U.S. 601 (1895).

ment gave the federal government control over matters traditionally reserved to the states. As such it might have had far-reaching influences upon our federal system, but the Twenty-first Amendment made it only a temporary diversion. Thus, only the Civil War Amendments, terminating slavery and subjecting the states to national oversight through the effectual veto power exercised by the Supreme Court over state legislation, seriously modified the distribution of power in our constitutional system. These Civil War Amendments apart, the emergence of national parties has had a more powerful influence on the workings of our government than any structural change.

To prevent the recurrence of abuses which had been manifest under English rule or under the Articles of the Confederation, or to quiet fears of the smaller states, the Constitution contains specific restrictions upon state and national power. For instance, the states are forbidden to impair the obligation of contract, to coin money, to lay tonnage duties, or to make treaties. Conversely, the federal government is forbidden to tax exports, or to lay a direct tax not apportioned according to population, or to give preference to the ports of any state. On the other hand, the federal government was given certain very definite powers: to coin money, for instance, and to declare war. But, as we have noted earlier, particularized provisions, just because they particularize, do not raise the thorny problems of construction. The really persistent and troublesome questions as to the distribution of power between state and nation arise in the application of the comprehensive clauses giving Congress the power "to regulate commerce . . . among the several states" and "to lay and collect taxes." They arise also from the implications of the fact that we are a union of states.

Inevitably, therefore, the interplay of forces within a federalism is largely moulded by judicial interpretation. And since the formulas to be applied, either as expressed in words in the Constitution or drawn out of its supposed presuppositions, are very flexible in scope, they leave wide freedom of opinion to individual judges. It makes all the difference how deeply one cares for assuring a free market throughout the country, or how discerningly one sees the economic interrelationships upon which the attainment of such a market depends. It makes all the difference how truly one cares that the states have the amplest opportunity for local development as to matters clearly beyond the legal powers of the nation. In sitting in judgment upon the attempts of others to meet the perplexities of society, it makes all the difference how aware one is of the complexity of modern economic problems and organic relation of abstractly unrelated transactions. In this as in other vital phases of constitutional interpretation, the determining factors are the judge's underlying conception of the Constitution and his awareness of the psychological problems presented when he sits in judgment upon the judgment of legislatures on issues outside the domain of logical demonstration.

Every legal system for a living society, even when embodied in a written constitution, must itself be alive. It is not merely the imprisonment of the past; it is also the unfolding of the future. Of all the means for ordering the political life of a nation, a federal system is the most complicated and subtle; it demands the most flexible and imaginative adjustments for harmonizing national and local interests. The Constitution of the United States is not a printed finality but a dynamic process; its application to the actualities of govenment is not a mechanical exercise but a function of statecraft.

Mr. Justice Holmes, therefore, never misconceived the nature of the enterprise in which the Court is engaged whenever it passes on the validity of legislation. Especially when the Court is asked to reject an act of Congress on the ground that it would disturb the balance between state and federal powers, the judicial judgment, as exercised by the Justice, brought into play precedents and the considerations that moulded them, history as reflected in speech and action of statesmen, above all, a just deference to the findings of Congress regarding contemporary economic circumstances and their organic relation to national needs for which Congress must provide. It would require his own originality to surmise with what Voltairian phrase the Justice would have exposed the ingenuousness of the Court's notion of what it was doing, when, early in 1936, it invalidated the Agricultural Adjustment Act. To the majority it was not unlike a simple problem of linear measurement. They deemed themselves called upon merely "to lay the article of the Constitution which is invoked beside the statute which is challenged and to decide whether the latter squares with the former."[3] How odd that would have sounded to one who, throughout his judicial life, insisted that

> . . . the provisions of the Constitution are not mathematical formulas having their essence in their form; they are organic living institutions transplanted from English soil. Their significance is vital not formal; it is to be gathered not simply by taking the words and a dictionary, but by considering their origin and the line of their growth.[4]

The Constitution created a national community, and the power given to Congress "to regulate Commerce . . . among the several States" has been the most fertile source of energy for promoting the idea that, though we are a federation of states, we are also a nation. Mr. Justice Holmes in memorable language summarized his own experience with the role actually played by the commerce clause:

> I do not think the United States would come to an end if we lost our power to declare an Act of Congress void. I do think the Union would be imperiled if we could not make that declaration as to the laws of the several States. For one in my place sees how often a local policy prevails with those who are not trained to national views and how often action is taken that embodies what the Commerce Clause was meant to end.[5]

This testimony is all the more impressive because the Justice was unusually jealous, as we shall see, that the

[3] United States v. Butler, 297 U.S. 1, 62 (1936).

[4] Gompers v. United States, 233 U.S. 604, 610 (1914), cited above, I, n. 10.

[5] Holmes, *Collected Legal Papers*, pp. 295–96.

states have the amplest opportunity for action touching those events which have their life peculiarly within their confines.

Until 1887, the national authority was exercised largely through the power of the Court to put brakes on state legislation that either discriminated against, or imposed undue burdens upon, a free national market. Beginning with the Interstate Commerce Act, the government intervened to affect commerce through positive legislation. The tide of Congressional legislation came in, as we have noted, just about the time that Mr. Justice Holmes joined the Court. The limit which in his view the Court could put upon Congress was merely an application of his general philosophy regarding judicial review.

The abstract legal issue raised by such legislation was not in dispute. The wisdom of a particular use of the commerce clause by Congress is for the judgment of Congress and not the Court's business; but the Congressional judgment must satisfy the Court's view regarding the power of Congress to entertain its judgment. Thus formulated in dry terms of abstract power, the problem is a constant temptation to word-spinning and self-deception. Legally, states and nation seem antithetic entities; economically, they are interacting forces. No matter how well screened by doctrinal phrases or sterilized principles, the cases arising under the commerce clause cover concrete conflicts of interests between state and national power. And the national power is mutilated or denied by distinctions that do not respond to the actualities of modern industry. Here, as elsewhere, Mr. Justice Holmes insisted that we "think things instead of words." To him, therefore, "commerce is not a technical legal conception, but a practical one, drawn from the course of business." From this practical conception he drew practical implications. When the majority found hindrance in the Constitution to legislation intended to prevent a recurrence of Pullman strikes and to promote industrial peace on railroads, he protested:

> It cannot be doubted that to prevent strikes, and, so far as possible, to foster its scheme of arbitration, might be deemed by Congress an important point of policy, and I think it impossible to say that Congress might not reasonably think that the provision in question would help a good deal to carry its policy along. But suppose the only effect really were to tend to bring about the complete unionizing of such railroad laborers as Congress can deal with, I think that object alone would justify the act. I quite agree that the question what and how much good labor unions do, is one on which intelligent people may differ,—I think that laboring men sometimes attribute to them advantages as many attribute to combinations of capital disadvantages, that really are due to economic conditions of a far wider and deeper kind—but I could not pronounce it unwarranted if Congress should decide that to foster a strong union was for the best interest, not only of the men, but of the railroads and the country at large.[6]

Strikes grow out of unsatisfactory industrial standards, and these are lifted through social legislation as well as by the power of collective bargaining. For a good many years an important disturbing factor in our economy has been the diversity of conditions of employment in differ-

[6] Adair v. United States, 208 U.S. 161, 191–92 (1908).

ent regions of the country the products of which compete in the same market. Business in one state considers itself handicapped if its rivals in another state are operating under less onerous requirements of industrial law, even though in the long view a depressed status for labor is not a wise economy. As a result, real obstructions are placed upon free movement across state lines; the social policy of progressive states is jeopardized by states pursuing more shortsighted aims. In 1916 Congress began to deal with this problem in its most appealing phase, namely, child labor. It subjected all products entering the flow of commerce across state lines to standards of employment consonant with modern notions regarding the protection of child life. A bare majority of the Court invalidated this act as a forbidden intrusion of Congress into state affairs. This opened a controversy that for twenty years has deflected much political effort and engendered needless ill-will. For the analysis which Mr. Justice Holmes made on behalf of the minority has not yet been answered in reason:

The objection urged against the power [to prohibit the shipment in interstate commerce of the products of manufacturing establishments employing child labor] is that the States have exclusive control over their methods of production and that Congress cannot meddle with them, and taking the proposition in the sense of direct intermeddling I agree to it and suppose that no one denies it. But if an act is within the powers specifically conferred upon Congress, it seems to me that it is not made any less constitutional because of the indirect effects that it may have, however obvious it may that it will have those effects, and that we are not at liberty upon such grounds to hold it void. . . . I should have thought that the most conspicuous decisions of this Court have made it clear that the power to regulate commerce and other constitutional powers could not be cut down or qualified by the fact that it might interfere with the carrying out of the domestic policy of any State. . . .

The act does not meddle with anything belonging to the States. They may regulate their internal affairs and their domestic commerce as they like. But when they seek to send their products across the state line they are no longer within their rights. If there were no Constitution and no Congress their power to cross the line would depend upon their neighbors. Under the Constitution such commerce belongs not to the States but to Congress to regulate. It may carry out its views of public policy whatever indirect effect they may have upon the activities of the States. Instead of being encountered by a prohibitive tariff at her boundaries the State encounters the public policy of the United States which it is for Congress to express. The public policy of the United States is shaped with a view to the benefit of the nation as a whole. If, as has been the case within the memory of men still living, a State should take a different view of the propriety of sustaining a lottery from that which generally prevails, I cannot believe that the fact would require a different decision from that reached in *Champion* v. *Ames.* Yet in that case it would be said with quite as much force as in this that Congress was attempting to intermeddle with the State's domestic affairs. The national welfare as understood by Congress may require a different attitude within its sphere from that of some self-seeking State. It seems to me entirely constitutional for Congress to enforce its understanding by all the means at its command.[7]

Still less would Mr. Justice Holmes allow the states,

[7] Hammer v. Dagenhart, 247 U.S. 251, 277–81 (1918).

by a perverted use of logic, to play the dog in the manger and block the United States from effectuating a national policy which depended upon agreement with other countries. He spoke for the Court in sustaining a treaty to protect migratory birds. But the reach of his opinion would extend to other assertions of the treaty-making power to enforce the civilized needs of the world of which the United States is a part:

It is said that a treaty cannot be valid if it infringes the Constitution, that there are limits, therefore, to the treaty-making power, and that one such limit is that what an act of Congress could not do unaided, in derogation of the powers reserved to the States, a treaty cannot do. . . .

Acts of Congress are the supreme law of the land only when made in pursuance of the Constitution, while treaties are declared to be so when made under the authority of the United States. . . . It is obvious that there may be matters of the sharpest exigency for the national well being that an act of Congress could not deal with but that a treaty followed by such an act could, and it is not lightly to be assumed that, in matters requiring national action, "a power which must belong to and somewhere reside in every civilized government" is not to be found. . . . The treaty in question does not contravene any prohibitory words to be found in the Constitution. The only question is whether it is forbidden by some invisible radiation from the general terms of the Tenth Amendment. We must consider what this country has become in deciding what that Amendment has reserved. . . .

Here a national interest of very nearly the first magnitude is involved. It can be protected only by national action in concert with that of another power. The subject matter is only transitorily within the State and has no permanent habitat therein. But for the treaty and the statute there soon might be no birds for any powers to deal with. We see nothing in the Constitution that compels the Government to sit by while a food supply is cut off and the protectors of our forests and our crops are destroyed. It is not sufficient to rely upon the States. The reliance is vain, and were it otherwise, the question is whether the United States is forbidden to act.[8]

While the abstractions of logic could secure for the states paralyzing authority over national interests, logic could be employed no less effectively to dry up all state power. As a matter of dialectic, the economic activities of the country may be proven unseverable. Modern inventions have extended enormously the scope of federal control, and as an exercise in ratiocination the commerce clause could absorb the states. But the purposes of our federalism must be observed, and adjustments struck between state and nation. Here Mr. Justice Holmes' fundamental philosophy in rejecting absolutes, his spirit of accommodation, his realization that life is the reconciliation of contradictories, served as fruitful instruments for constitutional adjudication:

In modern societies every part is related so organically to every other, that what affects any portion must be felt more or less by all the rest. Therefore, unless everything is to be forbidden and legislation is to come to a stop, it is not enough to show that, in the working of a statute, there is some tendency, logically discernible, to interfere with commerce or existing contracts.[9]

Taxation is another great activity of government

[8] Missouri v. Holland, 252 U.S. 416, 432–35 (1920).
[9] Diamond Glue Co. v. United States Glue Co., 187 U.S. 611, 616 (1903).

which has engaged the Court for more than a hundred years in a continuous process of adjusting state and national interests. In this field the basis for the Court's interference is not any explicit provision of the Constitution, like the commerce clause, but implications drawn from the mere fact of federalism. Since two governments have authority within the same territory, neither can be allowed to cripple the operations of the other by taxation. Therefore state and federal governments must avoid exactions which discriminate against each other or impose oppressive burdens. These legal doctrines have their roots in actuality. But they have been distorted by speculative refinements not reflecting the practicalities of government. The passing observation of Marshall that "the power to tax involves the power to destroy,"[10] has been treated as though it were an encyclical to be reverently applied by deductive reasoning. And so the range of wealth which the Court withdrew from the taxing power of the states and nation without any relation to the actual working of our federal system became more and more pervasive. This, too, at a time when the financial needs of all governments steadily mounted. Mr. Justice Holmes was himself caught in this web of unrealities.[11] But he also, more than a hundred years after Marshall uttered his famous dictum, with one pithy stroke gave it its intellectual *coup de grâce*: "The power to tax is not the power to destroy while this Court sits."[12] Dealing with

[10] McCulloch v. Maryland, 4 Wheat. 316, 431 (U.S. 1819).
[11] Gillespie v. Oklahoma, 257 U.S. 501 (1922).
[12] Panhandle Oil Co. v. Mississippi *ex rel.* Knox, 277 U.S. 218, 223 (1928).

the practicalities of taxation, the Court need not imprison itself or hamper government by abstract formulas. At this very term the Court, with accelerated pace, is retracing its steps to such an extent that a minority protested against overruling, *sub silentio*, a century of precedents.[13]

But where there was no intersection of federal and state authority—that is, in areas where if the states are denied power the nation also has none—Mr. Justice Holmes was loath to find a governmental vacuum. Such limitation upon state legislation without a corresponding freedom for federal action was, it will be recalled, the product of judicial exegesis of the Fourteenth Amendment. A major portion of Mr. Justice Holmes' opinions expressed his watchfulness of state interests against exuberant judicial restrictions. He had an artist's craving for perfection and sought it through an austere observance of the demands of judicial self-limitation. But profound concern for society was also involved. Captain Holmes of the Twentieth Massachusetts fought for the Union but he did not want to devitalize the states:

> There is nothing that I more deprecate than the use of the Fourteenth Amendment beyond the absolute compulsion of its words to prevent the making of social experiments that an important part of the community desires, in the insulated chambers afforded by the several States, even though the experiments may seem futile or even noxious to me and to those whose judgment I most respect.[14]

[13] James v. Dravo Contracting Co., 302 U.S. 134 (1937).
[14] Truax v. Corrigan, 257 U.S. 312, 344 (1921).

Along the whole gamut of legislative activity, the Supreme Court interposed its veto against state action in matters confessedly of local concern and derived from local experience. In over two hundred cases the Court used the Fourteenth Amendment to strike down state action.[15] In an effort to deal with their local problems forty-two states have offended—all but six small states—and solely on the basis of the vague language of the Fourteenth Amendment. Moreover the significant cases were decided always by a divided Court, almost invariably over the protest of its most distinguished minds. In about forty percent of these cases there were dissents, while in the ordinary private litigation of the Court less than ten per cent of the cases gave rise to differences. To be sure, the Court sustained more laws than it nullified. But during the last decade of Mr. Justice Holmes' service, more than a third of state legislation assailed under the Fourteenth Amendment fell foul of the due process clause. Merely as a matter of statistics this is an impressive mortality rate. But numbers alone do not tell the tale. All laws are not of equal importance; and a single decision may decide the fate of many measures. Thus the Adkins case, which passed only on the minimum wage law of the District of Columbia, in fact terminated minimum wage regulation in a dozen states. Finally, the inhibition of legislative effort beyond the strict limits of an adverse decision and, conversely, the shifting of legislative responsibility to the courts are influences not measurable by statistics.

[15] See Appendices I and II [omitted in this edition].

Such judicial control of the individualism of the states is an aspect of centralization too often overlooked. It is socially costly and often capricious: costly, because judicial nullification based on unexamined assumptions of policy stops experimentation at its source and bars needed increase to the fund of social knowledge through tests of trial and error; capricious, because it so often turns on the fortuitous circumstances which determine a majority decision, particularly in matters of fact and opinion not peculiarly within the professional competence of lawyers. Against this dangerous use of judicial power, Mr. Justice Holmes directed the power and originality of his pen in the myriad variety of instances which presented the same central issue. A few samples must suffice.

The glow of his protest against denying Pennsylvania the right to restrict the use of shoddy gave redolent significance to an otherwise drab controversy:

> If the Legislature of Pennsylvania was of opinion that disease is likely to be spread by the use of unsterilized shoddy in comfortables I do not suppose that this Court would pronounce the opinion so manifestly absurd that it could not be acted upon. If we should not, then I think that we ought to assume the opinion to be right for the purpose of testing the law. The Legislature may have been of opinion further that the actual practice of filling comfortables with unsterilized shoddy gathered from filthy floors was widespread, and this again we must assume to be true. It is admitted to be impossible to distinguish the innocent from the infected product in any practicable way, when it is made up into the comfortables. On these premises, if the Legislature regarded the danger as very great and inspection and tagging as in-

adequate remedies, it seems to me that in order to prevent the spread of disease it constitutionally could forbid any use of shoddy for bedding and upholstery.[16]

Again, when a majority of the Court curbed the efforts of Wisconsin to restrict tax evasion, Mr. Justice Holmes broke a vigorous lance on behalf of Wisconsin's right to translate into law her own not irrational view of human experience:

If the Fourteenth Amendment were now before us for the first time I should think that it ought to be construed more narrowly than it has been construed in the past. But even now it seems to me not too late to urge that in dealing with state legislation upon matters of substantive law we should avoid with great caution attempts to substitute our judgment for that of the body whose business it is in the first place, with regard to questions of domestic policy that fairly are open to debate.

The present seems to me one of those questions. I leave aside the broader issues that might be considered and take the statute as it is written, putting the tax on the ground of an absolute presumption that gifts of a material part of the donor's estate made within six years of his death were made in contemplation of death. If the time were six months instead of six years I hardly think that the power of the State to pass the law would be denied, as the difficulty of proof would warrant making the presumption absolute; and while I should not dream of asking where the line can be drawn, since the great body of the law consists in drawing such lines, yet when you realize that you are dealing with a matter of degree you must realize that reasonable men may differ widely as to the place where the line should fall. I think that our discussion should end if we admit, what I certainly be-

[16] Weaver v. Palmer Bros., 270 U.S. 402, 415–16 (1926).

lieve, that reasonable men might regard six years as not too remote. . . .

I am not prepared to say that the legislature of Wisconsin, which is better able to judge than I am, might not believe, as the Supreme Court of the State confidently affirms, that by far the larger proportion of the gifts coming under the statute actually were made in contemplation of death. I am not prepared to say that if the legislature held that belief, it might not extend the tax to gifts made within six years of death in order to make sure that its policy of taxation should not be escaped.[17]

For Mr. Justice Holmes society was more than bargain and business, and his mind was particularly passionate when he vindicated interests not represented by the items of a balance sheet. As a final illustration, therefore, let me quote from an opinion on behalf of the Court, in which he refused to confine New Jersey's power of control over the Passaic River within the frame of narrow private rights:

. . . it appears to us that few public interests are more obvious, indisputable and independent of particular theory than the interest of the public of a State to maintain the rivers that are wholly within it substantially undiminished, except by such drafts upon them as the guardian of the public welfare may permit for the purpose of turning them to a more perfect use. This public interest is omnipresent wherever there is a State, and grows more pressing as population grows. It is fundamental, and we are of the opinion that the private property of riparian proprietors cannot be supposed to have deeper roots. . . . The private right to appropriate is subject not only to the rights of lower owners but to the

[17] Schlesinger v. Wisconsin, 270 U.S. 230, 241–42 (1926).

initial limitation that it may not substantially diminish one of the great foundations of public welfare and health.

We are of the opinion, further, that the constitutional power of the State to insist that its natural advantages shall remain unimpaired by its citizens is not dependent upon any nice estimate of the extent of present use or speculation as to future needs. The legal conception of the necessary is apt to be confined to somewhat rudimentary wants, and there are benefits from a great river that might escape a lawyer's view. But the State is not required to submit even to an aesthetic analysis. Any analysis may be inadequate. It finds itself in possession of what all admit to be a great public good, and what it has it may keep and give no one a reason for its will.[18]

Mr. Justice Holmes brought to his work a sense of history. His traditions were founded not on fear but on knowledge, and his rejections came from knowledge, not from the blindness of prejudice. He left issues in the arena where they belong. He knew that judges in their way legislate, and therefore did not propose that they should undermine the legislature's power to legislate. He knew too much to believe that it was within his power to save, if it was within the power of the legislature to ruin. "I believe with Montesquieu," he said, "that if the chance of a battle—I may add, the passage of a law—has ruined a state, there was a general cause at work that made the state ready to perish by a single battle or a law."[19] Therefore, whenever he upheld, as he so often did, legislation in the substance of which he disbelieved, he exhibited the

[18] Hudson County Water Co. v. McCarter, 209 U.S. 349, 356–57 (1908).

[19] Holmes, *Collected Legal Papers*, p. 295.

judicial function at its purest. He transcended his own preferences, for he was the guardian of the country's past, present, and future. And so he was as modern when he ended his work as when he began it.

From the constitutional opinions of Mr. Justice Holmes there emerges the conception of a nation adequate to its national and international duties, consisting of federated states in their turn possessed of ample power for the diverse uses of a civilized people. He was mindful of the Union which he helped to preserve at Balls Bluff, Antietam, and Fredericksburg; he was equally alert to assure scope for the states upon which the Union rests. He would not, by sterile abstraction, paralyze federal power over commerce beyond states lines, nor hamper the states in grappling with their local problems by a provincial or partisan application of the Fourteenth Amendment. He found the Constitution equal to the needs of a great nation at war; but according to the same Constitution the individual must not be sacrificed to the Moloch of unworthy fear.

Serenely dwelling above the sound of passing shibboleths, Mr. Justice Holmes steadfastly refused to hearken to the din of the moment. But his humility was too deep to make him regard even the highest tribunal as a Grand Lama. Like all human institutions, the Supreme Court, he believed, must earn reverence through the test of truth.[20]

[20] See the Lincoln Day, 1898, address of Mr. Justice Brewer, *Government by Injunction* (1898), 15 Nat. Corp. Rep. 849: "It is a mistake to suppose that the Supreme Court is either honored or helped by being spoken of as beyond criticism. On the contrary, the life

No judge of the Supreme Court has done more to establish it in the consciousness of the people. Mr. Justice Holmes is built into the structure of our national life and has written himself into the slender volume of the literature of all time.

---

and character of its justices should be the objects of constant watchfulness by all, and its judgments subject to the freest criticism. The time is past in the history of the world when any living man or body of men can be set on a pedestal and decorated with a halo. True, many criticisms may be, like their authors, devoid of good taste, but better all sorts of criticism than no criticism at all. The moving waters are full of life and health; only in the still waters is stagnation and death."